Grammar Guide 2

Kathleen F. Flynn • Marilyn Rosenthal • Irwin Feigenbaum • Linda Butler

with contributions by
Michael Berman • John Chapman • Robin Longshaw • Cheryl Pavlik • Jane Sturtevant

Boston, Massachusetts   Burr Ridge, Illinois   Dubuque, Iowa   Madison, Wisconsin
New York, New York   San Francisco, California   St. Louis, Missouri
Bangkok   Bogotá   Caracas   Lisbon   London   Madrid   Mexico City
Milan   New Delhi   Seoul   Singapore   Sydney   Taipei   Toronto

McGraw-Hill
A Division of The McGraw·Hill Companies

CONNECT WITH ENGLISH: GRAMMAR GUIDE BOOK 2

Copyright © 1998 by the WGBH Educational Foundation and the Corporation for Public Broadcasting. All rights reserved. Printed in the United States of America. Except as permitted under the United States Copyright Act of 1976, no part of this publication may be reproduced or distributed in any form or by any means, or stored in a data base or retrieval system, without the prior written permission of the publisher.

This book is printed on acid-free paper.

domestic   4 5 6 7 8 9 0 QPD QPD 3 2 1 0
international   2 3 4 5 6 7 8 9 0 QPD QPD 3 2 1 0 9 8

ISBN 0-07-292769-0

Editorial director: Thalia Dorwick
Publisher: Tim Stookesberry
Development editor: Pam Tiberia
Marketing manager: Tracy Landrum
Production supervisor: Richard DeVitto
Print materials consultant: Marilyn Rosenthal
Project manager: Shannon McIntyre, Function Thru Form, Inc.
Design and Electronic Production: Function Thru Form, Inc.
Typeface: Frutiger
Printer and Binder: Quebecor Press Dubuque

Grateful acknowledgment is made for use of the following:
Still photography: Jeffrey Dunn, Ron Gordon, Judy Mason, Margaret Storm

Library of Congress Catalog Card No.: 97-75579

International Edition
Copyright © 1998. Exclusive rights by The McGraw-Hill Companies, Inc., for manufacture and export. This book cannot be re-exported from the country to which it is consigned by The McGraw-Hill Companies, Inc. The International Edition is not available in North America.

When ordering this title, use ISBN 0-07-115912-6.

Table of Contents

To The Teacher   v

A Visual Tour   vi

EPISODE 13 Job Hunting
Review *BE*: Present Tense, Affirmative and Negative Statements
Review *BE*: Present Tense, *Yes/No* Questions and Short Answers
Review *BE*: Present Tense, *Wh-* Questions and Answers

EPISODE 14 A Bad Day
Review *BE*: Past Tense, Affirmative and Negative Statements
Review *BE*: Past Tense, *Yes/No* Questions and Short Answers
Review *BE*: Past Tense *Wh-* Questions and Answers

EPISODE 15 A Night Out
Can and *Could* (Ability, Possibility)
Can You/Could You/Would You (Requests)
Can, *Could*, and *May* (Permission)

EPISODE 16 First Day of Class
Review: Direct Object Nouns and Pronouns
Direct Object Infinitives: Affirmative and Negative Statements
Direct Object Infinitives: *Yes/No* Questions and Short Answers

EPISODE 17 Casey at the Bat
Review: Present Continuous Tense, Affirmative and Negative Statements
Review: Present Continuous Tense, *Yes/No* Questions and Short Answers
Review: Present Continuous Tense, *Wh-* Questions and Answers

EPISODE 18 The Art Gallery
Review: Simple Present Tense, Affirmative and Negative Statements
Review: Simple Present Tense, *Yes/No* Questions and Short Answers
Review: Simple Present Tense, *Wh-* Questions and Answers

EPISODE 19 The Picnic
   Review: Count Nouns
   Review: Non-Count Nouns
   Sentences with *There Was/There Were*

EPISODE 20 Prejudice
   Review: Simple Past Tense, Affirmative and Negative Statements
      (Regular Verbs)
   Review: Simple Past Tense, *Yes/No* Questions and Short Answers
      (Regular Verbs)
   Review: Simple Past Tense, *Wh-* Questions and Answers (Regular Verbs)

EPISODE 21 A Difficult Decision
   Simple Present Tense, Affirmative and Negative Statements
      (Irregular Verbs)
   Simple Past Tense, *Yes/No* Questions and Short Answers (Irregular Verbs)
   Simple Past Tense, *Wh-* Questions and Answers (Irregular Verbs)

EPISODE 22 Guitar Lessons
   Should and Must: Affirmative and Negative Statements;
      Yes/No Questions and Short Answers
   Compound Sentences with *And*, *Too*, and *Either*
   Tag Questions with *BE, Should,* and *Can*

EPISODE 23 The Retirement Party
   The Future with *Will:* Affirmative and Negative Statements
   The Future with *Will: Yes/No* Questions and Short Answers;
      Wh- Questions
   Present Continuous Tense and Simple Present Tense for Future Meaning

EPISODE 24 The Phone Call
   HAVE TO: Present Tense, Affirmative and Negative Statements;
      Yes/No Questions and Short Answers
   HAVE TO: Past Tense, Affirmative and Negative Statements;
      Yes/No Questions and Short Answers
   Compound Sentences with *Or*

TO THE TEACHER

The primary goal of each *Grammar Guide* is to help students develop mastery of the grammatical structures found throughout the **Connect with English** video episodes. This introduction and the following visual tour provide important information on how each *Grammar Guide* and the corresponding video episodes can be successfully combined to teach English as a second or foreign language.

PROFICIENCY LEVEL:
Designed for beginning through high-intermediate students, *Grammar Guides 1-4* provide a systematic presentation of the basic structures and grammatical features of American English. Examples from the video episodes are used to illustrate grammatical structures in both presentation and practice.

Students at various proficiency levels can benefit from using the *Grammar Guides*. Lower-level students will find the *Grammar Guides* a valuable resource tool they can rely on to help them internalize the authentic language of the video. More advanced students will welcome the carefully sequenced review of the language and its connection to the video through numerous examples and practices.

LANGUAGE SKILLS
Grammar Guides 1-4 provide practice with the linguistic building blocks of the language. They give students an opportunity to analyze and review the structures through clear and simple grammar charts and explanations. Exercises are transparent and help students build from a receptive understanding of the grammar point to language production through controlled exercises and finally, free-writing, using the grammar point to talk about their own lives. The grammar charts and explanations are particularly helpful to students whose learning style relies on analysis and explanation. The opportunities for practice are useful to students who learn language inductively through observation and practice with the structures.

OPTIONS FOR USE
Each *Grammar Guide* can be used in a variety of different learning environments, including classroom, distance learning, tutorial, and/or independent study situations. Students can use *Grammar Guides 1-4* before or after they watch the corresponding video episode, to either preview or review critical structures and grammatical topics.

Grammar Guides 1-4 can easily be combined with other corresponding texts in the **Connect with English** print program. For classes with an emphasis on listening, *Video Comprehension Books 1-4* help students build listening comprehension skills and gain a clear understanding of the characters and story line in the video series. For classes with an emphasis on oral communication skills, *Conversation Books 1-4* contain a variety of pair, group, team, and whole-class activities based on important themes and events from each episode. Finally, there are 16 *Connections Readers* that offer students graded reading practice based on the **Connect with English** story. These readers also use the same grammatical scope and sequence found in *Grammar Guides 1-4*.

A Visual Tour of this Text

This visual tour is designed to introduce the key features of *Grammar Guide 2*. The primary focus of each *Grammar Guide* is to help students develop mastery of key grammatical structures and concepts. *Grammar Guide 2* corresponds to episodes 13-24 of *Connect with English*. The scope and sequence of the grammar points in this book are developmental; topics become more advanced as the chapters progress.

Grammar Charts
The **Grammar Chart** explains the grammar topic and acts as a model that students can refer to as they do the exercises.

Photos
Photos from the corresponding video episode are used to illustrate the meaning of the grammar point.

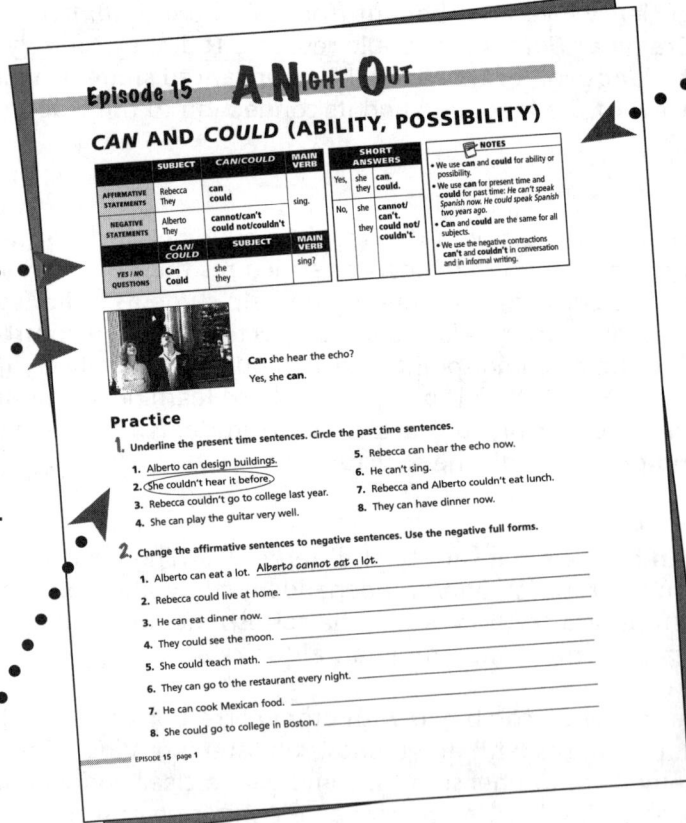

Notes
The **Notes** section offers additional explanations about the material being presented. These sections have been carefully worded so that the language of instruction is no more advanced than the grammatical structures being presented in the text.

Contextualized Exercises
The first exercise in the **Practice** section is always based on the characters, situations, and events that happen in the video. This first exercise is also usually on the receptive level, allowing students to recognize the structural point before they actually need to produce it.

Chapter Structure
Every episode of *Grammar Guide 2* presents three grammar points, each on a two-page spread. Each grammar presentation has the following features:
- A grammar chart, illustrating the structures or grammatical features;
- Simple explanatory usage notes;
- A photo from the video episode illustrating the context of the grammar point;
- A practice section of exercises taking the student from a receptive knowledge to productive practice with the structure;
- A more advanced practice (**Power Practice**) section providing the student with an opportunity for free writing about his/her own life using the target structure.

Guided Practice
Subsequent exercises in the **Practice** section provide students with an opportunity to further practice the structure. The task in each exercise increases slightly in difficulty throughout each lesson. Some of these exercises are focused on the video, and others are set in other real-world contexts. The language used in all exercises — in direction lines, examples, and the items themselves — is very simple and utilizes only the structures that have been introduced up to that point in the book.

Relating Grammar to Everyday Life
The **Power Practice** section allows a chance for students to use the target structure to write about things that are meaningful in their own lives. It's a particularly useful tool for multilevel classrooms, as it gives students an opportunity to produce language at a variety of different levels.

page vii

Episode 13 — Job Hunting

REVIEW *BE*: PRESENT TENSE, AFFIRMATIVE AND NEGATIVE STATEMENTS

AFFIRMATIVE STATEMENTS		AFFIRMATIVE CONTRACTIONS	NEGATIVE STATEMENTS			NEGATIVE CONTRACTIONS
SUBJECT	BE		SUBJECT	BE	NOT	
I	am	I'm	I	am		I'm not.
He / She / It	is	fine.	She	is	not	fine.	She's not. / She isn't.
		he's / she's / it's				
We / You / They	are	we're / you're / they're	We	are		We're not. / We aren't.

NOTES
- We use the present tense of **BE** for habits, routines, generalizations, and present situations.
- There are two negative contractions for each subject pronoun except **I**: *He's not late. / He isn't late. You're not late. / You aren't late.*
- We use contractions in conversation and in informal writing.

Rebecca: ***I'm*** fine, Kevin. Nancy**'s** great. Everything ***is*** OK.

Practice

1. Read the sentences below. Circle all the forms of the verb *BE*.

Rebecca (is) in San Francisco now. (She's) at her godmother's home. Nancy and Rebecca aren't alone in the house. There are two other people, Angela and Melaku. They're students, too. Right now, Rebecca is on the phone with her brother. Rebecca is happy. Everything is OK.

2. Change the full forms of *BE* to contractions.

1. I am Rebecca. *I'm Rebecca.*
2. He is Melaku. _____
3. She is Angela. _____
4. You are here. _____
5. We are students. _____
6. They are at home. _____
7. It is OK. _____
8. I am tired. _____

3. Complete the sentences with *am*, *is*, or *are*.

1. He __is__ old.
2. You _____ lucky.
3. She _____ in the kitchen.
4. I _____ at school.
5. It _____ in the car.
6. The books _____ here.

4. Change the sentences to negative statements. Use *isn't* or *aren't*.

1. He is my friend. He isn't my friend.

2. She is lazy. _____

3. We are sick. _____

4. It is expensive. _____

5. You are late. _____

5. Write affirmative sentences using words from the boxes.

I	We	am	Chinese.	tall and handsome.
He	You	is	from Mexico.	beautiful and smart.
She	They	are	a student.	28 years old.
It			married.	

1. They are Chinese.

2. _____

3. _____

4. _____

5. _____

6. _____

POWER Practice

6. Write about your things. Choose four things from the box. Write one negative and one affirmative statement about each one. Use contractions.

| books | TV | clothes | phone | keys | wallet |

Examples: My books aren't on my desk. They're in my bag.   My TV isn't big. It's small.

1. _____

2. _____

3. _____

4. _____

7. Write six affirmative statements and six negative statements about you and your family. Use contractions. Use your own paper.

Examples: I'm 22 years old.   My parents aren't here with me.

REVIEW *BE*: PRESENT TENSE, *YES/NO* QUESTIONS AND SHORT ANSWERS

YES/NO QUESTIONS		AFFIRMATIVE SHORT ANSWERS	NEGATIVE SHORT ANSWERS	📝 NOTES
BE	**SUBJECT**			• **BE** comes *before* the subject in **Yes/No** questions.
Am	I	I **am**.	I **am not**. / **I'm not**.	• We use [**Yes** or **No** + subject + **BE**] in short answers.
Is	he/she/it OK?	Yes, she **is**.	No, she **is not**. / **she's not**. / she **isn't**.	• We use contractions in conversation and in informal writing.
Are	we/you/they	we **are**.	we **are not**. / **we're not**. / we **aren't**.	

Is Rebecca at the college?

Yes, she **is**.

Practice

8. Match the *Yes/No* questions and their short answers. Write the letters.

1. __b__ Is Rebecca at the college?   a. No, she isn't.
2. _____ Is she in class?   ✔ b. Yes, she is.
3. _____ Are Rebecca and Maria in Maria's office?   c. Yes, they are.
4. _____ Is a job available for Rebecca?   d. Yes, she is.
5. _____ Is Rebecca upset at the news?   e. No, it isn't.

9. Write questions with *Am*, *Is*, or *Are*.

1. you / OK Are you OK?   4. he / from Mexico _____
2. we / late _____   5. they / musicians _____
3. the class / here _____   6. college / expensive _____

10. Complete the short answers to the questions.

1. Is Rebecca in San Francisco? Yes, _she is._
2. Is Nancy's house big? Yes, _____
3. Is Nancy a young woman? No, _____
4. Are Angela and Melaku music students? No, _____
5. Is college cheap? No, _____

11. Change the statements to *Yes/No* questions. Write short answers. Use contractions in negative short answers.

1. We're not hungry.   Are you hungry?   No, we aren't.
2. I'm a new student.   _____   _____
3. They're not in class.   _____   _____
4. He's from Korea.   _____   _____
5. We aren't tired.   _____   _____

12. Use the words in the boxes to write *Yes/No* questions. Write short answers to the questions.

Is	an elephant	ants	small	fast
Are	a mouse	bears	big	tall
	a lion		strong	

1. Is an elephant big?   Yes, it is.
2. _____   _____
3. _____   _____
4. _____   _____
5. _____   _____

Power Practice

13. Write *Yes/No* questions about places. Use *Is* and *Are*. Write short answers to the questions.

Examples: Is Tokyo expensive? Yes, it is. (or) Are the Rocky Mountains in Africa? No, they aren't.

1. _____
2. _____
3. _____
4. _____
5. _____

14. Write six *Yes/No* questions and short answers about people in your family. Use the adjectives in the box. Use your own paper.

| beautiful | funny | handsome | kind | married | talented | tall |

Examples: Is my brother tall? Yes, he is. (or) Are my uncles married? No, they aren't.

REVIEW BE: PRESENT TENSE, WH- QUESTIONS AND ANSWERS

WH- QUESTION WORD	BE	SUBJECT	ANSWERS
Who	are	they?	They're my friends.
What	is	it?	It's a message.
Where	are	the books?	They're on the table.

NOTES
- The question word **Who** asks about people.
- The question word **What** asks about things, places, or ideas.
- The question word **Where** asks about places.
- We use [**Wh-** question word + **'s**] for singular subjects in conversation and in informal writing: *Who's that man? What's that? Where's the car?* We don't use **'re** with **Wh-** question words.

Where are Rebecca and Nancy?

They're in the kitchen.

Practice

15. Match the *Wh-* questions and their answers. Write the letters.

1. __d__ Who's Nancy Shaw?
2. _____ Where is Nancy's house?
3. _____ What's her uncle's name?
4. _____ Who are Melaku and Angela?

a. It's in San Francisco.
b. They are students.
c. It's Edward.
✔d. She's Rebecca's godmother.

16. Complete each question with *Who*, *What*, or *Where*.

1. __Where__ is the newspaper?
   It's on the table.
2. __What__ is that?
   It's a surprise.
3. __Who__ is that woman?
   She's my aunt.
4. __Where__ are my glasses?
   Next to the phone.
5. __Who__ are those boys?
   My cousins.
6. __What__ is her name?
   It's Mary.

17. Write the questions.

1. who / that girl   Who is that girl?
2. where / your home   _____
3. what / their names _____
4. who / those people _____

18. Read the incomplete statements. Write questions about the missing information. Use **Who**, **What**, and **Where**.

1. My family is in . . . <u>Where is your family?</u>

2. His name is . . . _____

3. Their house is on . . . _____

4. She is my . . . _____

5. The keys are in the . . . _____

19. Write questions about the people and things in the box. Use **Who**, **What**, or **Where** + **is** or **are**.

| Madonna | the Big Apple | Cinderella |
| the Sunshine State | the Twin Cities | the White Mountains |

1. <u>What is the Sunshine State?</u>

2. _____

3. _____

4. _____

5. _____

6. _____

POWER Practice

20. PRETEND: You are at a party with a friend. The people and the place are new to you. Ask your friend questions. Use **Who**, **What**, or **Where** + **is** or **are**.

Examples: Who is that handsome man? What is in that room? Where are the other people?

1. _____

2. _____

3. _____

4. _____

5. _____

21. PRETEND: You have new neighbors. Write four questions about these people. Use **Who**, **What**, and **Where**. Use your own paper.

Examples: Who is she? Where are they from?

Episode 14 — A Bad Day

REVIEW *BE*: PAST TENSE, AFFIRMATIVE AND NEGATIVE STATEMENTS

AFFIRMATIVE STATEMENTS			NEGATIVE STATEMENTS				NEGATIVE CONTRACTIONS	
SUBJECT	BE		SUBJECT	BE	NOT			
I / He / She / It	was	late.	I / He / She / It	was	not	late.	I / He / She / It	wasn't.
We / You / They	were		We / You / They	were			We / You / They	weren't.

NOTES
- We use the past tense of **BE** for past situations.
- There are no *affirmative* contractions for **was** or **were**.
- We use the negative contractions **wasn't** and **weren't** in conversation and in informal writing.

It was a bad day for Rebecca.
She wasn't lucky.

Practice

1. Check (✔) the sentences with the past tense forms of *BE*.

1. ✔ It was a bad day for Rebecca.
2. ___ A job is important to her.
3. ___ There aren't many good part-time jobs.
4. ✔ Rebecca wasn't successful today.
5. ___ Job interviews are difficult.
6. ✔ One interview was very upsetting for Rebecca.

2. Circle the correct past form of *BE*: *was* or *were*.

1. I (was)/ were absent yesterday.
2. The weather (was)/ were beautiful last week.
3. We was /(were) not at home yesterday evening.
4. My grades was /(were) very good last year.
5. It (was)/ were not cold last night.
6. The boys was /(were) at the beach all day.
7. You was /(were) a big help. Thank you.
8. I (was)/ were happy to meet him.

3. Write sentences about the story. Use *was* or *were*.

1. Mr. Casey / a firefighter — Mr. Casey was a firefighter.
2. Nancy's uncle / a musician — Nancy's uncle was a musician
3. Rebecca's last job / in a factory — Rebecca's last job was in a factory
4. Rebecca's interviews / disappointing — Rebecca's interviews were disapointing
5. Rebecca and Angela / in the living room — They's were in the living room

4. Rewrite the sentences in the past. Use contractions.

1. We aren't lucky. — We weren't lucky.
2. He isn't successful. — he wasn't successful
3. They aren't married. — The weren't married
4. I'm not surprised. — I wasn't surprised
5. You're not happy. — You weren't happy
6. It's not difficult. — It's wasn't difficult

POWER Practice

5. Complete the sentences. Choose a subject. Use *wasn't* or *weren't*.

Examples: My birthday present wasn't a surprise.
These exercises weren't difficult.

1. My quizz - wasn't _____ difficult.
2. he wasn't speak _____ fun.
3. They weren't _____ a surprise.
4. _____ interesting.
5. _____ a problem.
6. _____ expensive.

6. Write five sentences about your past. Use the time expressions in the box. Use your own paper.

| last night | three days ago | last year | yesterday | last weekend | in 1995 |

Examples: I was in bed at 9:00 last night.
I was a student in 1995.

REVIEW *BE*: PAST TENSE, *YES/NO* QUESTIONS AND SHORT ANSWERS

YES/NO QUESTIONS			AFFIRMATIVE SHORT ANSWERS			NEGATIVE SHORT ANSWERS			NOTES
BE	SUBJECT								• **BE** comes *before* the subject in **Yes/No** questions.
Was	I he she it	late?	Yes,	I he she it	was.	No,	I he she it	was not. wasn't.	• We use [**Yes** or **No** + subject + **BE**] in short answers.
Were	we you they			we you they	were.		we you they	were not. weren't.	• We use the negative contractions **wasn't** and **weren't** in conversation and in informal writing.

Was the phone call for Rebecca?
Yes, it was.

Practice

7. Circle the correct short answer.

1. Was Rebecca surprised at Alberto's phone call?   (Yes, she was.) / Yes, it is.
2. Was she upset about the phone call?   No, he isn't. / No, she wasn't.
3. Was Alberto interested in Rebecca?   Yes, he was. / Yes, she is.
4. Was Rebecca ready for a date?   No, she wasn't. / No, it isn't.
5. Were Nancy and Melaku there?   No, they aren't. / No, they weren't.

8. Write *Yes/No* questions with *Was* or *Were*.

1. you / sick   Were you sick?
2. we / late   Were we late?
3. I / noisy   Was I noisy?
4. she / happy   Was she happy?
5. he / tired   Was he tired?
6. you / hungry   Were you hungry?
7. they / rich   Were they rich?
8. it / easy   Was it easy?

EPISODE 14   page 3

9. Complete the short answers to these questions about the story. Use full forms or contractions.

1. Was the phone call for Angela? No, it was not. (or) No, it wasn't.
2. Were Kevin and Mr. Casey on the phone? No, They weren't on the Phone
3. Was the call from Alberto? Yes, he was
4. Was Rebecca surprised at the call? Yes, she was surprised at the call
5. Were Angela and Melaku friendly to Alberto? Yes, They were friendly to albert

10. Change the statements to *Yes/No* questions. Write short answers.

1. Albert Einstein wasn't an artist. Was Albert Einstein an artist? No, he wasn't.
2. Cleopatra was an Egyptian queen. Was she an egyptian queen? yes, she was
3. Washington and Lincoln were American presidents. Were they American Presiden? No, They weren't
4. Queen Victoria wasn't from France. Was she Queen from France? No, she wasn't
5. Michelangelo and Donatello weren't musicians. Were they musicans? No, he weren't

POWER Practice

11. Write *Yes/No* questions about you and your friends. Use *Was* or *Were*. Use the place and time expressions in the boxes. Write short answers to your questions.

| in school | at a party | at home | last night | two days ago |
| at work | at the movies | | yesterday | last weekend |

Examples: Were Paolo and Rosa at the movies last night? Yes, they were.

1. was Mary at a party? yes, she was
2. were Bilhan and I at the movies last weekend? yes, we were
3. was Arturo at work yesterday? No, he wasn't
4. were you at home last night? No, I weren't
5. were we in school two days ago? Yes, we were.

12. Write five *Yes/No* questions about you and your family. Use *Was* or *Were*. Use the adjectives in the box. Write short answers to your questions. Use your own paper.

| happy | tired | bored | upset | ready |

Examples: Was I bored last weekend? Yes, I was. (or) Were my brothers ready for their exams? No, they weren't.

EPISODE 14 page 4

REVIEW BE: PAST TENSE, WH- QUESTIONS AND ANSWERS

WH- QUESTION WORD	BE	SUBJECT	ANSWERS	NOTES
Who	was	he?	He **was** my grandfather.	• We use [**Wh–** question word + **was** or **were** + subject] for past tense information questions.
What	was	that noise?	It **was** a fire alarm.	
When	was	the accident?	It **was** yesterday.	• The question word **When** asks about time, days, or dates.
Where	were	the boys?	They **were** in the park.	

Where were Rebecca and Alberto?
In the hall at Nancy's house.

Practice

13. Circle the correct **Wh-** question word.

1. What /(Who)/ When was Rebecca's date? Alberto.
2. Where / What / When was Rebecca and Alberto's date? In the evening.
3. Who / When / Where was Alberto's car? Outside the house.
4. When / Who / What was Alberto's secret? A surprise gift for Rebecca.

14. Match the **Wh-** questions and their answers. Write the letters.

1. __d__ Who was Margaret Casey?   a. In Boston.
2. __a__ Where was Rebecca's last job?   b. Last June.
3. __c__ What were her job responsibilities?   c. She was a factory supervisor.
4. __b__ When was Kevin's graduation?   ✓d. She was Rebecca's and Kevin's mother.

15. Write questions. Use **was** or **were**.

1. who / the Incas   Who were the Incas?
2. when / the last summer Olympics   _____
3. who / Mahatma Gandhi   _____
4. where / the first World Cup games _____
5. what / the Titanic   _____

16. Write questions with *Who* or *What*.

1. Who was Spanky? _____ Spanky was our cat.
2. _____ The girl's name was Aya.
3. _____ Mr. and Mrs. Ruiz were our neighbors.
4. _____ The problem was a dead car battery.
5. _____ The star of the film was Jackie Chan.
6. _____ The date yesterday was August 15.

17. Write questions with *When* or *Where*.

1. When was the baseball game? _____ The baseball game was last Saturday.
2. _____ The accident was on Main Street.
3. _____ The wedding was in June of last year.
4. _____ We were at the movies last night.
5. _____ Our exams were last week.
6. _____ The meeting was in Room 101.

POWER Practice

18. **PRETEND:** Your friend was at a party. Write five *Yes/No* and five *Wh-* questions about the party.

Examples: Where was the party? Was it fun?

1. _____
2. _____
3. _____
4. _____
5. _____
6. _____
7. _____
8. _____
9. _____
10. _____

Episode 15 — A Night Out

CAN AND COULD (ABILITY, POSSIBILITY)

	SUBJECT	CAN/COULD	MAIN VERB
AFFIRMATIVE STATEMENTS	Rebecca / They	can / could	sing.
NEGATIVE STATEMENTS	Alberto / They	cannot / can't / could not / couldn't	
	CAN / COULD	SUBJECT	MAIN VERB
YES / NO QUESTIONS	Can / Could	she / they	sing?

SHORT ANSWERS		
Yes,	she / they	can. / could.
No,	she / they	cannot / can't. / could not / couldn't.

NOTES
- We use **can** and **could** for ability or possibility.
- We use **can** for present time and **could** for past time: *He can't speak Spanish now. He could speak Spanish ten years ago.*
- **Can** and **could** are the same for all subjects.
- We use the negative contractions **can't** and **couldn't** in conversation and in informal writing.

Can she hear the echo?
Yes, she **can**.

Practice

1. Underline the present time sentences. Circle the past time sentences.

1. <u>Alberto can design buildings.</u>
2. (She couldn't hear it before.)
3. Rebecca couldn't go to college last year.
4. She can play the guitar very well.
5. Rebecca can hear the echo now.
6. He can't sing.
7. Rebecca and Alberto couldn't eat lunch.
8. They can have dinner now.

2. Change the affirmative sentences to negative sentences. Use the negative full forms.

1. Alberto can eat a lot. _Alberto cannot eat a lot._
2. Rebecca could live at home. _____
3. He can eat dinner now. _____
4. They could see the moon. _____
5. She could teach math. _____
6. They can go to the restaurant every night. _____
7. He can cook Mexican food. _____
8. She could go to college in Boston. _____

EPISODE 15 page 1

3. Complete the short answers. Use *can't* or *couldn't*.

1. Can Alberto speak Chinese? No, _he can't._
2. Could Ramón go to college? No, _____
3. Can Alberto's father retire now? Yes, _____
4. Can Rebecca cook Mexican food? No, _____
5. Could Alberto go to college? Yes, _____
6. Could Rebecca buy a new car? No, _____

POWER Practice

4. Write six sentences about your family members. Use *can* or *can't*.

Examples: My sisters can cook Italian food.
My brothers can't swim.

1. _____
2. _____
3. _____
4. _____
5. _____
6. _____

5. Write six sentences about you. What *can/can't* you do now? What *could/couldn't* you do five years ago?

Examples: I can drive a car.
I couldn't drive a car five years ago.

1. _____
2. _____
3. _____
4. _____
5. _____
6. _____

CAN YOU/COULD YOU/WOULD YOU (REQUESTS)

CAN/ COULD/ WOULD	SUBJECT	PLEASE	(NOT)	MAIN VERB
Can Could Would	you	please		help me? speak English?
			not	laugh?

> **NOTES**
> - We use [**can/could/would** + **you**] for requests: *Can you tell me the time?*
> - We use **can** for polite requests. We use **could** and **would** for very polite requests.
> - We use **please** to make *any* request more polite: *Would you please speak more slowly?*
> - We use **not** for negative requests. We ask someone **not** to do something: *Could you not feed the goldfish?*

Rebecca: **Could** you **please not** walk so fast?

Practice

6. Put a check next to the requests.

1. ____ Can you read Spanish?
2. ✔ Can you give me the menu?
3. ____ Would you sit down?
4. ____ Could you please not leave?
5. ____ Could you hand me the salt?
6. ____ Can Alberto's mother cook very well?
7. ____ Would you please get me some coffee?
8. ____ Could Ramón get a different job?

7. Change these affirmative requests to negative requests.

1. Would you please use a lot of salt? *Would you please not use a lot of salt?*
2. Could you please talk? _____
3. Would you please ask me about it? _____
4. Can you open the door? _____

8. Put the words in the correct order.

1. sing / please / me / for / you / would   *Would you please sing for me?*
2. coat / hold / you / my / can   _____
3. could / stand / you / here   _____
4. can / not / you / look / at / me   _____

9. Match the situations with the requests.

Situations

1. __e__ I need a pencil.
2. ____ I can't read this.
3. ____ I need a dime.
4. ____ You sing very well.
5. ____ I have a cold.

Requests

a. Could you lend me a dime?
b. Would you bring me an aspirin?
c. Would you sing another song?
d. Can you read this to me?
✔ e. Would you please give me a pencil?

Power Practice

10. PRETEND: You are riding in a crowded bus. Write three affirmative requests. Write three negative requests.

Examples: Would you please move your coat? Could you please not push?

Affirmative Requests

1. _____
2. _____
3. _____

Negative Requests

1. _____
2. _____
3. _____

11. PRETEND: You are the parent of a teenage child. Write three affirmative requests. Write three negative requests.

Examples: Would you please do your homework? Could you please not watch TV now?

Affirmative Requests

1. _____
2. _____
3. _____

Negative Requests

1. _____
2. _____
3. _____

CAN, COULD, AND MAY (PERMISSION)

	SUBJECT	CAN/COULD/MAY	MAIN VERB	SHORT ANSWERS			NOTES
AFFIRMATIVE STATEMENTS	Rebecca They We	can could may	go now.	Yes,	she they we	can. could. may.	• We use **can**, **could**, and **may** for permission. • **Can** is informal. **Could** is formal. **May** is very formal. • We use **can** for permission *very* often in conversation and in informal writing. • **Can**, **could**, and **may** are the same for all subjects.
NEGATIVE STATEMENTS	Alberto They We	cannot/can't could not/couldn't may not		No,	she they we	cannot. can't. could not. couldn't. may not.	
	CAN/COULD/MAY	SUBJECT	MAIN VERB				
YES / NO QUESTIONS	Can Could May	she they we	go now?				

Alberto: **May** I kiss you?

Practice

12. Check (✔) the informal sentences.

1. ✔ You can have anything on the menu.
2. ✔ You could talk with your client.
3. ✔ You can have dessert.
4. ✔ Can I order for you?
5. ___ Yes, you may.
6. ___ May I take your coat?

13. Put the words in the correct order.

1. could / dessert / Rebecca / have   *Rebecca could have dessert.*
2. to / the / restaurant / come / Alex / may   _____
3. dinner / Rebecca / pay / for / not / may   _____
4. leave / can / for / a / minute / Alberto   _____
5. on / Saturdays / in / the / restaurant / can / help / Alex   _____
6. Mrs. Mendoza / talk / about / may / not / Alberto's / dates   _____

14. Change the negative statements to affirmative statements.

1. You can't sing here. _You can sing here._
2. She couldn't sing her mother's song. _____
3. He may not hold Rebecca's hand. _____
4. They cannot have dinner now. _____
5. Rebecca can't meet Alberto's parents. _____

POWER Practice

15. PRETEND: Your child is going to Disneyland. Write three affirmative permission statements. Write three negative permission statements. Use *can*, *could*, or *may*.

Examples: You can stay all day.   You may not go alone.

Affirmative Permission Statements

1. _____
2. _____
3. _____

Negative Permission Statements

1. _____
2. _____
3. _____

16. PRETEND: You are in a new English class. Write *Yes/No* questions for permission and answer them. Use *can*, *could*, or *may*.

Examples: May we write in pencil? Yes, you may.

Yes/No Questions	Short Answers
1. _____	_____
2. _____	_____
3. _____	_____
4. _____	_____
5. _____	_____
6. _____	_____

Episode 16 — First Day of Class

REVIEW: DIRECT OBJECT NOUNS AND PRONOUNS

SUBJECT	VERB	DIRECT OBJECT NOUN
We	want	a job. a car. a resume. friends. clothes. help. money.
Rebecca	wants	

SUBJECT	VERB	DIRECT OBJECT PRONOUN
The Caseys	like	me. us. you. them. him. her. it.
Rebecca	likes	

NOTES
- Direct object nouns and pronouns follow the main verb in a sentence.
- We use the object form of pronouns as direct objects.

Professor Thomas teaches **music**.
Professor Thomas teaches **it**.

Practice

1. Underline the direct object nouns. Circle the direct object pronouns.

1. Rebecca and Bill study <u>music</u>.
2. Rebecca and Bill study (it).
3. Maria helps Rebecca.
4. Maria helps her.
5. Rebecca meets Alex and Vincent.
6. Rebecca meets them.
7. Rebecca watches Professor Thomas.
8. Rebecca watches him.

2. Change the direct object nouns to direct object pronouns.

1. She fixes the car.   *She fixes it.*
2. He reads the letters. _____
3. Yuri calls Sarah. _____
4. The doctor examines Pedro. _____
5. They clean the room. _____
6. She sees Mr. Chu and me. _____

3. Read Rebecca's letter to Kevin. Write the correct direct object pronoun in each space below.

Dear Kevin,

I started music school today. I love ____it____ . María Gómez, the financial aid officer,
(1)

helped me with a payment plan. I thanked _____ . Today I also talked to the
(2)

director of an after-school program. She interviewed _____ . Then I played with
(3)

some of the children there. I liked _____ a lot.
(4)

How's Dad? Do you help _____ ? He needs _____ .
(5)   (6)

I miss _____ .
(7)

Love,

Rebecca

POWER Practice

4. Write five sentences about your life. Use a direct object noun in each sentence.

Example: I play football.

1. _____
2. _____
3. _____
4. _____
5. _____

5. Write five sentences about you and your friends or family. Use direct object pronouns.

Example: My brother: He helps me. My parents: I love them.

Person	Sentence
1. _____	_____
2. _____	_____
3. _____	_____
4. _____	_____
5. _____	_____

DIRECT OBJECT INFINITIVES: AFFIRMATIVE AND NEGATIVE STATEMENTS

	SUBJECT	MAIN VERB	DIRECT OBJECT INFINITIVE	
AFFIRMATIVE STATEMENTS	They	plan	**to study**	tomorrow.
	She	likes	**to work**	with children.
NEGATIVE STATEMENTS	They	don't plan	**to practice**	tomorrow.
	He	doesn't like	**to work**	with children.

NOTES
- A direct object infinitive follows the main verb in the sentence.
- A direct object infinitive is [**to** + the simple form of the following verb].
- A direct object infinitive can also have words after the second verb: *We want to see the movie.*
- Some common verbs with direct object infinitives are: *begin, decide, forget, hate, hope, learn, like, love, need, plan, promise, refuse, remember, start,* and *want.*

Rebecca needs **to start** a payment program.

Practice

6. Circle the direct object infinitives.

Some people want (to buy) the Casa Mendoza Restaurant. Alberto wants to sell the restaurant. But Ramón refuses to sell it. He loves to work there, and he doesn't want to lose the family business. Alberto plans to have a family meeting. Ramón drives away. He needs to pick up Alex at the after-school program.

7. Check (✔) the sentences with direct object infinitives.

1. ✔ I'm learning to drive a car.
2. ___ We begin the semester tomorrow.
3. ___ Would you please remember to close the door?
4. ___ Pam decided to go to the party.
5. ___ Elena refused the invitation.
6. ___ Michael didn't want to make dinner.
7. ___ He's not planning to take a vacation.
8. ___ Don't forget to put gas in the car!

8. Put the words in the correct order.

1. love / read / long / to / I / books — I love to read long books.
2. to / she / Panama / travel / to / plans — *she travel to Panama by Plans*
3. he / to / week / last / started / practice — *he started to practice to last week*
4. didn't / my / do / to / remember / I / homework
5. need / tomorrow / they / to / work / don't
6. promised / house / we / paint / to / the
7. is / she / refusing / apartment / her / leave / to

9. Write sentences with direct object infinitives. Use words from the box.

| to work | to go | to make | to take | to study |

1. We want __to work__ in the store.
2. She promised _____ in the library.
3. I decided _____ to the restaurant.
4. He needs _____ more money.
5. You forgot _____ your check.

POWER Practice

10. PRETEND: You are the leader of your country. Write five sentences for a speech. Use direct object infinitives.

Example: I promise to build new roads.

1. _____
2. _____
3. _____
4. _____
5. _____

11. Write five sentences about the people in your family. Use direct object infinitives. Use your own paper.

Example: My mother likes to work in the garden.

DIRECT OBJECT INFINITIVES: *YES/NO* QUESTIONS AND SHORT ANSWERS

YES/NO QUESTIONS

DO/DOES/DID	SUBJECT	MAIN VERB	DIRECT OBJECT INFINITIVE	
Do	they	want	**to go**	to the movies?
Does	he	plan	**to take**	a vacation?
Did	you	remember	**to call**	your mother?

SHORT ANSWERS

YES/NO	SUBJECT	DO/DOES/DID (+ NOT)
Yes,	they	do.
No,	they	don't.
Yes,	he	does.
No,	he	doesn't.
Yes,	I	did.
No,	I	didn't.

NOTES

- **Yes/No** questions take **do/does/did** before the subject of the sentence.
- Short answers take [**Yes/No** + subject + **do/does/did** (+ **not**).]
- We use the negative contractions **don't**, **doesn't**, and **didn't** in conversation and in informal writing.

Bill: **Do you want to meet** in the student lounge in an hour?

Practice

12. **A.** Read the sentences below. Underline *do/does/did* and the *subject*. Circle the *main verb*. Draw a box around the *direct object infinitive*.

1. Does Rebecca (want) to study with Bill?
2. Do Bill and Rebecca need to work hard?
3. Did Rebecca refuse to work with Emma?
4. Does Alberto hope to sell the restaurant?
5. Did Rebecca like to play with the children?
6. Did the Mendozas decide to sell the restaurant?

B. Match the short answers below to the questions above.

a. __1__ Yes, she does.   d. _____ Yes, she did.
b. _____ Yes, he does.   e. _____ No, she didn't.
c. _____ No, they didn't. f. _____ Yes, they do.

13. Complete the questions with the main verb and the direct object infinitive.

1. (like, eat) Do you _like to eat_____ spicy food?

2. (learn, use) Did you _____ direct object pronouns?

3. (love, study) Does she _____ grammar?

4. (plan, take) Did they _____ the test?

14. Look at the questions and short answers below. Complete the spaces with **Do**, **Does**, or **Did** and the *subject pronoun*.

1. <u>Do you</u> like to go to art galleries?   Yes, I do.
2. _____ remember to buy milk?   Yes, I did.
3. _____ plan to go to the meeting?   No, they don't.
4. _____ promise to teach him?   No, she didn't.
5. _____ need to come to class every day?   No, he doesn't.

15. Answer the questions below with short answers.

1. Did you learn to cook from your mother?   <u>Yes, I did. (or) No, I didn't.</u>
2. Do you like to dance?
3. Does your friend love to play games with you?
4. Did you begin to study English this year?
5. Do your parents plan to retire soon?
6. Did your government promise to lower taxes?

POWER Practice

16. What do you want to know about your teacher? Write five questions to ask him or her. Use object infinitives.

Example: Do you like to give difficult exams?

1. _____
2. _____
3. _____
4. _____
5. _____

17. PRETEND: Who is your favorite famous person? Write five questions to ask him or her. Use direct object infinitives. Use your own paper.

Example: Do you plan to write another book soon?

Episode 17 — CASEY AT THE BAT

REVIEW: PRESENT CONTINUOUS TENSE, AFFIRMATIVE AND NEGATIVE STATEMENTS

AFFIRMATIVE STATEMENTS	
SUBJECT + BE	MAIN VERB + -ING
I **am** / I**'m**	
She **is** / She**'s**	working.
We **are** / We**'re**	

NEGATIVE STATEMENTS	
SUBJECT + BE + NOT	MAIN VERB + -ING
I **am not** / I**'m not**	
She **is not** / She**'s not**/She **isn't**	working.
We **are not** / We**'re not**/We **aren't**	

NOTES
- We use the present continuous tense for actions in progress now, at the time of speaking.
- Affirmative statements in the present continuous tense use [subject + **BE** + main verb + **-ing**]
- Negative statements in the present continuous tense use [subject + **BE** + **not** + main verb + **-ing**]
- The present continuous tense uses the same full forms and contractions as the present tense with **BE**.
- Another name for the present continuous tense is the present progressive tense.

Alex: *I'm waiting* for my dad.

Practice

1. Underline the verbs in the present continuous tense.

Rebecca has a new job. She's <u>working</u> at an after-school program. Right now, the children are going home. It's late afternoon, and the program is finished for the day. Rebecca isn't working at the moment. She's talking with Alex. They're sitting together on the stairs. Alex is waiting for his father.

2. Write *am*, *is*, or *are*.

1. I ____am____ making a phone call.
2. They _____ playing tennis.
3. She _____ studying.
4. We _____ relaxing.
5. It _____ lying on the table.
6. I _____ having a cup of coffee.
7. He _____ getting a haircut.
8. You _____ doing a good job.

3. Change these statements from affirmative to negative. Use either form of the negative contractions.

1. I am having fun. _I'm not having fun._
2. They are washing the car. _____
3. She is riding her bicycle. _____
4. You are studying. _____
5. It is taking a long time. _____
6. We are getting old. _____

4. Write affirmative statements in the present continuous tense. Use contractions.

1. you / smile _You're smiling._
2. they / sleep _____
3. he / run / in a race _____
4. we / play / cards _____
5. I / try _____

5. Write one negative statement and one affirmative statement in the present continuous tense for each situation below. Use the verbs in the box.

| talk | read | cook | study | eat | listen | sit | watch |

1. I'm at school. _I'm not watching the clock. I'm listening to the teacher._
2. He's in the kitchen. _____
3. They're in the living room. _____
4. We're at a restaurant. _____
5. She's on the bus. _____
6. You're in the library. _____

POWER Practice

6. Where are you? What are you doing? Write eight sentences about you. Use the present continuous tense. Use your own paper.

Examples: I'm sitting at my desk. I'm wearing jeans and a shirt. I'm not drinking anything.

REVIEW: PRESENT CONTINUOUS TENSE, YES/NO QUESTIONS AND SHORT ANSWERS

YES/NO QUESTIONS			AFFIRMATIVE SHORT ANSWERS		NEGATIVE SHORT ANSWERS		NOTES
BE	**SUBJECT**	**MAIN VERB + -ING**		I **am**.		I **am not**. I'm **not**.	• We use [**BE** + subject + main verb + **-ing**] in **Yes/No** questions in the present continuous tense.
Am	I		Yes,	she **is**.	No,	she **is not**. she's **not**./she **isn't**.	• The short answers for **Yes/No** questions are the same in the present continuous tense and in the present tense with **BE**.
Is	he/she/it	working?		we **are**.		we **are not**. we're **not**./we **aren't**.	
Are	we/you/they						

Is Mr. Casey feeling well? **No, he isn't.**

Practice

7. Check (✔) the *Yes/No* questions in the present continuous tense.

1. _____ Is Mr. Casey at home?
2. ✔ Is he talking on the phone?
3. _____ Is he speaking with Rebecca?
4. _____ Is Kevin there?
5. _____ Are Rebecca and her father talking about his health?
6. _____ Is Mr. Casey feeling OK?

8. Match the *Yes/No* questions and their answers. Write the letters.

1. _c_ Is Rebecca having a hard time in school?   a. No, they aren't.
2. _____ Is Rebecca studying math?   b. Yes, it is.
3. _____ Are the children playing outside?   ✔c. Yes, she is.
4. _____ Are the children learning about tennis?   d. Yes, they are.
5. _____ Is Alex playing baseball?   e. No, she's not.
6. _____ Is Rebecca's job going well?   f. Yes, he is.

9. Change the statements to *Yes/No* questions. Write short answers. Use either form of the contractions in negative short answers.

1. I'm not doing my homework. <u>Are you doing your homework? No, I'm not.</u>

2. The children are swimming. _____

3. We're not eating. _____

4. The TV isn't working. _____

5. He's fixing his car. _____

10. Write *Yes/No* questions in the present continuous tense.

1. the boys / play / outside   <u>Are the boys playing outside?</u>

2. the doctor / speak / to the patient   _____

3. you / work / part time   _____

4. the neighbors / give / a party   _____

5. I / make / too much noise   _____

POWER Practice

11. Write short answers to the questions below.

Examples: *Are you sitting down now? Yes, I am. (or) No, I'm not.*

1. Are you sitting down now? _____

2. Are you holding a pen? _____

3. Are you learning English? _____

4. Are you studying at home? _____

5. Are your friends studying English? _____

6. Are you using a computer now? _____

12. What are you doing right now? What is happening around you? Write five *Yes/No* questions and short answers. Use the present continuous tense. Use your own paper.

Examples: *Am I sitting at my desk? Yes, I am. (or) Is the radio playing? No, it isn't.*

REVIEW: PRESENT CONTINUOUS TENSE, *WH-* QUESTIONS AND ANSWERS

WH- QUESTION WORD	BE	SUBJECT	MAIN VERB + -ING	ANSWERS
Who / Whom	are	you	calling?	My friend.
What	is	he	doing?	He's sleeping.
Where	are	they	living?	In Texas.

NOTES
- We use [**Who, Whom, What,** or **Where,** + **BE** + subject + main verb + **-ing**] in present continuous **Wh-** questions.
- We use [**Wh-** question word + **'s**] for singular subjects in conversation and in informal writing: *Who's she calling? What's he doing? Where's she going?*
- We use **Who** in conversation and in informal writing. We use **Whom** in formal writing and in formal speaking.

What is Rebecca **doing**? She's talking to Emma Washington.

Practice

13. Check (✔) the *Wh-* questions in the present continuous tense.

1. ✔ Where are Rebecca and Emma standing?
2. ____ What are they doing?
3. ____ Where is Ramón?
4. ____ What are the children playing?
5. ____ Is Ramón looking at Rebecca?
6. ____ What is he thinking?

14. Circle the correct *Wh-* question word.

1. Who / (What) / Where   is he studying?   Computer science.
2. Who / What / Where   are they getting married?   At City Hall.
3. Who / What / Where   are you eating?   Spaghetti.
4. Who / What / Where   is she talking to?   Her sister.
5. Who / What / Where   is the movie playing?   At the mall.
6. Who / What / Where   are they building?   A new school.

15. Write questions in the present continuous tense. Use the words below.

1. who / she / marry — Who is she marrying?
2. what / they / do _____
3. where / you / live _____
4. who / he / argue / with _____
5. what / she / wear / today _____
6. where / you / go _____

16. Read the incomplete statements. Write **Wh-** questions about the missing information.

1. The teacher is speaking to . . . — Who is the teacher speaking to?
2. They're working at . . . _____
3. The baby is eating . . . _____
4. We're buying . . . _____
5. My parents are living in . . . _____
6. I'm inviting . . . _____

POWER Practice

17. PRETEND: You are talking to your friend on the phone. Your friend is in the kitchen. Ask your friend questions with **Who**, **What**, and **Where**. Use the present continuous tense or the present tense of **BE**.

Examples: What are you doing? Who are you with?

1. _____
2. _____
3. _____
4. _____
5. _____

18. PRETEND: It's Saturday evening, and you are at home. You are sick in bed. You are thinking about your friends. Write four **Wh-** questions and four **Yes/No** questions about them. Use the present continuous tense. Use your own paper.

Examples: What is Teresa doing? Are my friends having fun?

Episode 18 — The Art Gallery

REVIEW: SIMPLE PRESENT TENSE, AFFIRMATIVE AND NEGATIVE STATEMENTS

AFFIRMATIVE STATEMENTS			NEGATIVE STATEMENTS			
SUBJECT	MAIN VERB		SUBJECT	DO/DOES + NOT	MAIN VERB	
I / We / You / They	work.		I / We / You / They	do not / don't	work.	
	watch	TV.			watch	TV.
	have	fun.			have	fun.
	do	a good job.				
	go	fast.				
He / She / It	works.		He / She / It	does not / doesn't	do	a good job.
	watches	TV.				
	has	fun.			go	fast.
	does	a good job.				
	goes	fast.				

NOTES

- We use the simple present tense for:
  — present situations.
  — permanent facts.
  — repeated actions.
  — generalizations.
  — events in a story.
- We use the simple form of the verb for **I**, **we**, **you**, and **they**. We add **-s** or **-es** to the verb after **he**, **she**, or **it**.
- The verbs **have**, **do**, and **go** are irregular. Their forms are: **have/has**; **do/does**; and **go/goes**.

Ramón: *Christine is moving to L.A. She **wants** Alex.*

Mrs. Mendoza: *Oh no! Alex **belongs** here. You **need** each other.*

Practice

1. Underline the verbs in the present continuous tense. Circle the verbs in the simple present tense.

Ramón <u>is talking</u> with his mother. He (has) a letter from his ex-wife. She and her new husband are moving to Los Angeles. They want Alex. Ramón feels terrible. He's telling his mother about the letter. They're talking about the problem. She gives Ramón her advice. Alex doesn't know about the problem yet.

2. Circle the correct form of the simple present tense.

1. Ramón have / (has) a son.
2. Alex live / lives with his father.
3. He see / sees his mother on weekends.
4. Ramón and Alex love / loves each other.
5. Ramón do / does his best for his son.
6. Alex don't / doesn't like L.A.

3. Complete these affirmative statements in the simple present tense. Use the verbs in parentheses ( ).

1. (live) We ___live___ on a quiet street.
2. (speak) They _____ Spanish.
3. (do) She _____ the housework.
4. (go) He _____ fishing.
5. (do) You _____ a good job.
6. (have) She _____ one sister.

4. Rewrite these statements in the negative. Use contractions.

1. You look tired. _You don't look tired._
2. He has a big apartment. _____
3. I need a haircut. _____
4. She goes to school by bus. _____
5. We do the shopping on Saturdays. _____

5. Write affirmative or negative statements about the story. Use the simple present tense.

1. Mr. and Mrs. Mendoza / have / a restaurant   _Mr. and Mrs. Mendoza have a restaurant._
2. Alberto / not / work / at the restaurant   _Alberto does not work at the restaurant._
3. the restaurant / serve / Mexican food   _____
4. it / not / serve / breakfast   _____
5. Ramón and his parents / run / the restaurant   _____

POWER Practice

6. Write six facts about a friend. Use the simple present tense. Write affirmative and negative statements. Use these verbs: **go, have, like, live, speak, work.**

Examples: My friend Omar lives in New York. He doesn't have a car.

1. _____
2. _____
3. _____
4. _____
5. _____
6. _____

7. Write facts about you. Use the simple present tense. Write four affirmative statements and four negative statements. Use your own paper.

Examples: I have a good job. I don't live in Canada.

REVIEW: SIMPLE PRESENT TENSE, *YES/NO* QUESTIONS AND SHORT ANSWERS

QUESTIONS			SHORT ANSWERS					NOTES
DO/DOES	SUBJECT	MAIN VERB	AFFIRMATIVE			NEGATIVE		
Do	I / we / you / they	work?	Yes,	I / we / you / they	do.	No,	I / we / you / they	do not. / don't.
Does	he / she / it			he / she / it	does.		he / she / it	does not. / doesn't.

NOTES
- We use [**Do/Does** + subject + the simple form of the main verb] in **Yes/No** questions in the simple present tense.
- In short answers with **Yes**, we use [subject + **do/does**]
- In short answers with **No**, we use [subject + **do/does** + **not**]
- We use the negative contractions **don't** and **doesn't** in conversation and in informal writing.

Does Rebecca **know** about Alberto's surprise? **No, she doesn't.**

Practice

8. Check (✔) the *Yes/No* questions in the simple present tense.

1. ____ Are Rebecca and Alberto looking at photographs?
2. ✔ Does Alberto have a surprise for Rebecca?
3. ____ Are many photos hanging on the walls at the gallery?
4. ____ Do Alberto and Rebecca look at all the pictures?
5. ____ Is Rebecca having a good time?
6. ____ Does Rebecca like Alberto's surprise?

9. Complete the short answers. Use contractions in negative short answers.

1. Do you have a camera? Rebecca: *No,* **I don't.**
2. Do you like photography? Alberto: *Yes,* _____
3. Does Rebecca go to many art galleries? Alberto: *No,* _____
4. Does Alberto take good photos? Rebecca: *Yes,* _____
5. Do you know many people at the gallery? Rebecca: *No,* _____
6. Do many people look at Rebecca's photo? Alberto: *Yes,* _____

10. Write *Yes/No* questions in the simple present tense.

1. he / play / the guitar — Does he play the guitar?
2. you / want / some coffee _____
3. she / understand / the problem _____
4. they / have / umbrellas _____
5. it / snow / in the winter _____

11. Change these statements to *Yes/No* questions. Write short answers. Use contractions in negative short answers.

1. She doesn't like cats. Does she like cats? No, she doesn't.
2. I live with my parents. _____
3. He works downtown. _____
4. They don't know their neighbors. _____
5. It doesn't hurt much. _____

12. Write *Yes/No* questions about people in the story. Use the simple present tense. Use the verbs in the box.

Examples: Do Rebecca and Alberto like each other? Does Ramón have a big problem?

have	know	like	need	work

1. _____   4. _____
2. _____   5. _____
3. _____   6. _____

POWER Practice

13. Write ten *Yes/No* questions about your friends and your family. Use the simple present tense. Use the verbs in the box. Write short answers to your questions. Use your own paper.

Examples: Does my friend Yoshi have a nice car? Yes, he does.
Do my parents live in the city? No, they don't.

have	live	know	like	need	work	go	do	wear	give

EPISODE 18 page 4

REVIEW: SIMPLE PRESENT TENSE, WH- QUESTIONS AND ANSWERS

WH-QUESTION WORD	DO/DOES	SUBJECT	MAIN VERB	ANSWERS
Who / Whom	do	they	like?	Elizabeth.
What	do	you	do?	I'm a bus driver.
When	does	he	eat?	At 6:00 p.m.
Where	does	she	work?	In a bank.

NOTES
- We use [**Wh-** question word + **do/does** + subject + verb] for information questions in the simple present tense.
- We use **Who** in conversation and in informal writing. We use **Whom** in formal writing and in formal speaking.

Where do the Mendozas **meet**? At the restaurant.

Practice

14. Circle the correct *Wh-* question word.

1. Who / What /(Where) do the Mendozas have their meeting? At the restaurant.
2. What / When / Where does Alberto have in mind? A plan to sell the restaurant.
3. Who / What / When does Alberto argue with? Ramón.
4. What / When / Where do Ramón and Alex go? To a picnic.
5. Who / When / Where does Alberto dance with his mother? After the meeting.

15. Write *Who*, *What*, *When*, or *Where*.

1. _Who_ do they have for their teacher? Mr. Thompson.
2. _____ does she go on vacation? To the beach.
3. _____ do they play baseball? After school.
4. _____ do you want for dinner? Mexican food.
5. _____ does she write to? Her boyfriend.
6. _____ does he do? He's a dentist.

16. Write **Wh-** questions in the simple present tense.

1. what / he / study   What does he study?
2. where / you / go to school _____
3. when / we / have classes   _____
4. who / you / meet for lunch _____
5. what / she / do after class _____

17. Mark is a college student. Read the incomplete sentences about him. Write **Wh-** questions about the missing information. Use the simple present tense.

1. Mark studies . . .   What does Mark study?
2. He takes classes at . . .   _____
3. His classes meet on . . .   _____
4. He does his research at . . . _____
5. Mark studies with . . .   _____

POWER Practice

18. PRETEND: You have a new friend. Ask your friend about his or her job. Write **Wh-** questions in the simple present tense. Use the words in the box.

Examples: Where do you work? Who do you work with?

do	eat lunch	work	start work

1. _____
2. _____
3. _____
4. _____
5. _____

19. PRETEND: Your neighbor is studying English. Write four **Wh-** questions and four **Yes/No** questions for your neighbor. Use the simple present tense. Use your own paper.

Examples: Where do you go to school? Do you like it?

Episode 19  The Picnic

REVIEW: COUNT NOUNS

REGULAR COUNT NOUNS			
SINGULAR		PLURAL	
a	book		books
an	egg	some	eggs
one	car	two	cars
the	box	a lot of	boxes

IRREGULAR COUNT NOUNS			
SINGULAR		PLURAL	
a	tooth		teeth
the	child	the	children
one	foot	a few	feet
a	woman	some	women
one	man	two	men
one	person	ten	people
		her	clothes

NOTES
- We can count some nouns: *one car, two cars*. We call these **count nouns**.
- Many count nouns are *regular*. They form plurals with **-s** or **-es**: *book, books; box, boxes*.
- Some count nouns are *irregular*. They form plurals in other ways: *woman, women; man, men*.
- Some count nouns are always plural: *clothes; scissors; jeans*.

They had some **hot dogs** and **hamburgers** on the grill.

PRACTICE

1. Underline the singular count nouns. Circle the plural count nouns.

1. Alex and Vincent won the race.
2. The children had fun.
3. One boy ate four hot dogs.
4. Two boys hurt Vincent.
5. There is an invitation for Rebecca.
6. Vincent's clothes were dirty.

2. Complete the sentences with *a*, *an*, or *many*.

1. Many people don't like picnics.
2. My father has _____ successful business.
3. Yoko has _____ invitation to the party.
4. They are visiting _____ countries in Asia.
5. My sister has _____ English class.
6. We go to _____ parties at Christmas time.

SPELLING RULES FOR PLURAL COUNT NOUNS	
RULES AND EXAMPLES	
Most nouns (*book, chair*) →	Add **–s** to the singular form: *books, chairs*
Most nouns ending in *–s, –z, –sh, –ch, –ss* or *–x* (*class, box*) →	Add **–es**: *classes, boxes*
Some nouns ending in *–o* (*tomato, potato*) →	Add **–es**: *tomatoes, potatoes*
Some nouns ending in *–y* (*country, party*) →	Remove **–y** and add **–ies**: *countries, parties*
Some nouns ending in *-fe* or *f* (*wife, leaf*) →	Change the **f** to **v** and add **–s** or **–es**: *wives, leaves*

3. Write the correct singular or plural form of the count nouns in the chart. Use (—) in a space with no singular form.

Singular	Plural	Singular	Plural
1. wife	wives	7.	jeans
2. —	clothes	8. picnic	
3. life		9.	sandwiches
4. business		10.	tomatoes
5. dictionary		11. country	
6.	hamburgers	12. knife	

4. Look around your room. What do you see now? Write six sentences.

Examples: *I see one desk. I see four books and two dictionaries.*

1. _____
2. _____
3. _____
4. _____
5. _____
6. _____

5. Describe your town or city. Write six sentences. Use your own paper.

Examples: *My town has three restaurants.*
My town has a big university.

REVIEW: NON-COUNT NOUNS

NON-COUNT NOUNS			
—	food	a glass of	juice
the	information	a box of	cereal
some	time	a pound of	sugar
a lot of	money	a cup of	coffee
a piece of	paper	a lot of	work

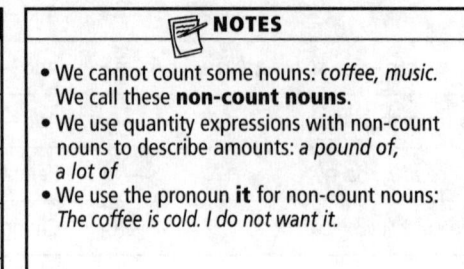

NOTES
- We cannot count some nouns: *coffee, music*. We call these **non-count nouns**.
- We use quantity expressions with non-count nouns to describe amounts: *a pound of, a lot of*
- We use the pronoun **it** for non-count nouns: *The coffee is cold. I do not want it.*

They had enough **food** for ten picnics.

6. Underline the non-count nouns. Circle the count nouns.

1. There is a lot of <u>food</u> in the (kitchen).
2. The children like fruit juice.
3. Everyone is having fun.
4. They didn't spend a lot of money.
5. The picnic was a lot of work.
6. They are bringing potato salad and potato chips.

7. Complete the sentences with *a/an* or *a lot of*.

1. He didn't give me __a lot of__ information about the trip.
2. _____ big car costs _____ money.
3. She can't go to _____ movie. She has _____ homework.
4. Please do the work quickly. I don't have _____ time.
5. We have _____ fruit. Would you like _____ apple or _____ pear?
6. My daughter drinks _____ milk.

8. Rewrite the sentences with the pronoun *it* in place of the non-count noun.

1. Do you have the information? _Do you have it?_
2. I am doing my homework. _____
3. They have the time. _____
4. He is cooking rice. _____
5. We don't have your money. _____

9. Complete the conversations with the words in the box. Use each word only once.

| butter | ✓coffee | eggs | homework | letters | mail | snow | soup | weather |

1. a. Let's make some _coffee_____.

   b. That's a good idea. I'm very tired and I can't go to sleep now. I have a lot of _____.

2. a. How is the _____ today?

   b. It's fine now, but we're going to get about five inches of _____ later.

3. a. We never get _____.

   b. Well, today is special. We got three _____!

4. a. Please buy one pound of _____ and some _____.

   b. We also need _____. We only have one more can.

POWER Practice

10. Make a shopping list. Write five count nouns and five non-count nouns. Use your own paper.

	Count Nouns	Non-Count Nouns
Examples:	eggs	milk

11. What does your country produce? What doesn't your country produce? Write six sentences about your country and its products. Use the words in the box. You can also use other words. Use your own paper.

| cars | cheese | clothes | coffee | corn | emeralds | gold |
| oil | pineapples | rice | shoes | steel | wheat | wine |

Examples: My country produces oil. My country doesn't produce rice.

SENTENCES WITH *THERE WAS/THERE WERE*

AFFIRMATIVE STATEMENTS		
THERE	**WAS/WERE**	**SUBJECT**
There	was	a pen. some milk. — milk.
	were	some boys. two books. a lot of people.

NEGATIVE STATEMENTS		
THERE	**WAS/WERE + NOT**	**SUBJECT**
There	was not wasn't	a pen. any milk. — milk. a lot of noise.
	were not weren't	any boys. two books. a lot of girls.

NOTES
- We use **There was** for singluar count nouns and for non-count nouns: *There was a book on the table. There was water in the glass.*
- We use **There were** for plural count nouns: *There were five people.*
- We use [There was/There were + **some**] in affirmative statements.
- We use [There wasn't/There weren't + **any**] in negative statements.

There were a lot of children in the race.

Practice

12. Underline *There was*. Circle *There were*.

1. There was a picnic in the park.
2. There were a lot of children at the picnic.
3. There was some trouble at the picnic.
4. (There was) enough food at the picnic.
5. There were hamburgers and hot dogs.
6. There were parents in the park.
7. There were many trees in the park.
8. There was a baseball field in the park.

13. Complete the sentences with *There was* or *There were*.

1. _____ some milk in the refrigerator this morning.
2. _____ a lot of students in the class yesterday.
3. _____ a pen on his desk.
4. _____ three mistakes on your test.
5. _____ some weather information on the television.
6. _____ a lot of snow last year.

14. Change these sentences from affirmative to negative.

1. There were some students in the classroom. <u>There weren't any students in the classroom.</u>
2. There was some food in the refrigerator. _____
3. There was some milk on the table. _____
4. There were two pens in her purse. _____
5. There was a lot of money on the table. _____
6. There were five people in the house. _____

15. Write sentences with words from the boxes.

There	was	two	seven	chairs	students	in the nest	in her pocket
	were	a lot of	two	money	trees	near the door	on the table
	wasn't	some	any	fruit	picnic	on Saturday	at my house
	weren't		a		bird	in front of the house	

1. <u>There were two chairs near the door.</u>
2. _____
3. _____
4. _____
5. _____
6. _____

Power Practice

16. Take a walk with a friend. Then write six sentences about your walk. Use affirmative and negative statements with *There was/There were*. Use your own paper.

Examples: There were a lot of cars on the street.
There weren't any children.

17. Do you remember your first English class? Write six sentences about it. Use affirmative and negative statements with *There was/There were*. Use your own paper.

Examples: There was a lot of conversation.
There wasn't any music in the class.

Episode 20 Prejudice

REVIEW: SIMPLE PAST TENSE, AFFIRMATIVE AND NEGATIVE STATEMENTS (REGULAR VERBS)

AFFIRMATIVE STATEMENTS		
SUBJECT	MAIN VERB	
I We You They He She It	arrived worked	yesterday.

NEGATIVE STATEMENTS			
SUBJECT	DID + NOT	MAIN VERB	
I We You They He She It	did not didn't	arrive work	yesterday.

NOTES
- We use the simple past tense for actions, habits, and generalizations in the past.
- We add **-ed** or **-d** to the simple form of the main verb for *regular verbs* in affirmative statements.
- We use [**did not/didn't** + the simple form of the main verb] in negative statements.

Officer Jones: *Those boys **attacked** Vincent. He **didn't start** the fight.*

Practice

1. Underline the verbs in the simple past tense.

Emma Washington <u>invited</u> Officer Jones to the after-school program. Officer Jones is a policewoman. She asked the children about the incident at the picnic. The children talked about the attack on Vincent. Officer Jones explained the meaning of "hate crimes." She surprised the children. One child asked, "Do you mean—it's against the law?"

2. Circle the correct verb. Choose the simple present or the simple past tense.

1. The play starts / (started) yesterday.
2. World War II ends / ended in 1945.
3. Whales live / lived in the ocean.
4. Dinosaurs don't exist / didn't exist now.
5. People don't use / didn't use computers in the 1800s.

3. Change these statements to the simple past tense.

1. I use a black pen. _I used a black pen._
2. It doesn't rain much. _____
3. We don't need help. _____
4. They work in the library. _____
5. He walks the dog. _____

4. Write statements about the story. Use the simple past tense.

1. a police officer / visit / the school.   A police officer visited the school.
2. she / talk / about the attack on Vincent   _____
3. Vincent / not / cause / the trouble   _____
4. Officer Jones / not / laugh / about the incident   _____
5. the children / agree / with her   _____

POWER Practice

5. Write affirmative and negative statements about your friends and family. Use the simple past tense. Use the verbs in the box.

Examples: My friends didn't call me last night.   My grandfather liked action movies.

call	graduate	like	listen	play	miss	watch	stay

1. _____
2. _____
3. _____
4. _____
5. _____
6. _____

6. Think about last weekend. Write four affirmative statements and four negative statements about your activities. Use the simple past tense of the verbs in the box. Use your own paper.

Examples: I cleaned my bedroom.   I didn't study Saturday night.

clean	fix	listen	walk	wash	cook	study	watch	work

REVIEW: SIMPLE PAST TENSE, *YES/NO* QUESTIONS AND SHORT ANSWERS (REGULAR VERBS)

YES/NO QUESTIONS			AFFIRMATIVE SHORT ANSWERS			NEGATIVE SHORT ANSWERS			NOTES
DID	SUBJECT	MAIN VERB	YES	SUBJECT	DID	NO	SUBJECT	DID + NOT	• We use [**Did** + subject + the simple form of the main verb] in **Yes/No** questions in the simple past tense. • We use [subject + **did**] in short answers with **Yes**. • We use [subject + **did** + **not** or **didn't**] in short answers with **No**.
Did	I we you they he she it	work	yesterday?	Yes,	I we you they he she it	did.	No,	I we you they he she it	did not. didn't.

Did Emma **talk** about prejudice? **Yes, she did.**

Practice

7. Check (✔) the *Yes/No* questions with *Did* in the simple past tense.

1. ✔ Did the children talk about the attack on Vincent?
2. ____ Did Emma ask questions?
3. ____ Were the children interested?
4. ____ Was Emma's talk about differences between people?
5. ____ Did she explain the meaning of the word "prejudice"?
6. ____ Did the children worry about Vincent's feelings?

8. Match the *Yes/No* questions and their short answers.

1. _d_ Did Emma talk about differences between people?   a. Yes, they did.
2. ____ Did the children listen?   b. Yes, they do.
3. ____ Were Rebecca and Alex there?   c. No, he wasn't.
4. ____ Was Vincent there?   ✔ d. Yes, she did.
5. ____ Did he stay home?   e. Yes, they were.
6. ____ Do the children miss Vincent?   f. Yes, he did.

9. Change these simple past tense statements to *Yes/No* questions. Write short answers.

1. I liked the movie. Did you like the movie? Yes, I did.
2. It didn't snow last night. _____
3. They fixed our computer. _____
4. She didn't need a ride. _____
5. He played the piano. _____
6. He didn't live in Miami. _____
7. It didn't happen yesterday. _____
8. They studied hard. _____

10. Write *Did, Was,* or *Were*.

1. Did _____ you pass the course?
2. _____ he excited about the news?
3. _____ she like the flowers?
4. _____ you on time?
5. _____ they wash the car?
6. _____ we too noisy?

11. PRETEND: Today was your friend's first day at a new job. Write past tense *Yes/No* questions for your friend.

Example: you / (use) a computer *Did you use a computer?*

1. you / (learn) new things _____
2. you / (be) very busy _____
3. your boss / (be) nice _____
4. your co-workers / (seem) friendly _____
5. you / (enjoy) your first day _____

POWER Practice

12. Think about your early childhood. Write ten past tense questions. Ask an older relative or family friend your questions. Write five questions with regular verbs from the box. Write five questions with *Was* or *Were*. Use your own paper.

Examples: Did I play with dolls? Were my brothers good to me?

| talk | enjoy | learn | like | play | watch | walk |

REVIEW: SIMPLE PAST TENSE, WH- QUESTIONS AND ANSWERS (REGULAR VERBS)

WH- QUESTION WORD	DID	SUBJECT	MAIN VERB	ANSWERS
Who / Whom	did	he	help?	Me.
What		you	study?	Math.
When		she	call?	Last night.
Where		they	work?	In a store.

NOTES
- We use [Wh– question word + **did** + subject + the simple form of the main verb] for simple past information questions.
- We use **Who** in conversation and in informal writing. We use **Whom** in formal writing or in formal speaking.

What did the children **make**? Cards for Vincent.

Practice

13. Circle the correct *Wh-* question word.

1. Who / (What) / When did Vincent want? — He wanted to be with his friends.
2. Who / What / Where did Vincent want to go? — To the after-school program.
3. What / When / Where did the children work on? — Some cards for Vincent.
4. What / When / Where did they work on the cards? — After Emma's talk.
5. Who / What / When did Alex miss? — Vincent.

14. Write *Who*, *What*, *When*, or *Where*.

1. <u>When</u> did World War I end? — In 1918.
2. _____ did Marco Polo travel? — To China.
3. _____ did Galileo discover? — The moons of Jupiter.
4. _____ did Napoleon marry in 1796? — Josephine.
5. _____ did Ludwig van Beethoven die? — In 1827.
6. _____ did Neil Armstrong walk? — On the moon.

15. Write *Wh-* questions in the simple past tense.

1. where / the famous writer / live — Where did the famous writer live?
2. what / the chef / cook _____
3. when / the plane / land _____
4. where / the race / start _____
5. who / you / vote for _____

16. Write past tense *Wh-* questions about the story. Ask about the information in parentheses ( ).

1. Rebecca lived (in Boston). Where did Rebecca live?
2. She worked (at a factory). _____
3. She worked with (her friend Sandy). _____
4. Rebecca dreamed about (a career in music). _____
5. She arrived in San Francisco (a little while ago). _____

POWER Practice

17. PRETEND: There was a party at your co-worker's house. It was a surprise for somebody. Write *Wh-* questions and *Yes/No* questions about the party. Use the verbs in the box.

Examples: *When did you invite the guests? Did people dance?*

| invite | cook | surprise | enjoy | dance | listen | end |

1. _____
2. _____
3. _____
4. _____
5. _____

18. PRETEND: You missed a phone call. Write six past tense questions about the call. Write *Wh-* questions and *Yes/No* questions. Use the verbs in the box or use *Was* or *Were*. Use your own paper.

Examples: *Did you answer the phone? Who did they want? Was it for me?*

| answer | ask | learn | call | need | want | talk |

EPISODE 20 page 6

Episode 21 — A Difficult Decision

SIMPLE PAST TENSE, AFFIRMATIVE AND NEGATIVE STATEMENTS (IRREGULAR VERBS)

SIMPLE FORM	SIMPLE PAST TENSE FORM
bring	brought
feel	felt
get	got
give	gave
hurt	hurt
make	made
put	put
say	said
see	saw
sleep	slept
speak	spoke
tell	told

AFFIRMATIVE STATEMENTS

SUBJECT	SIMPLE PAST TENSE FORM
I / We / You / They / He / She / It	slept.

NEGATIVE STATEMENTS

SUBJECT	DID + NOT	SIMPLE FORM OF THE VERB
I / We / You / They / He / She / It	did not / didn't	sleep.

NOTES
- The simple past tense of irregular verbs uses [subject + irregular past tense form] in affirmative statements. *They wrote letters.*
- We use [subject + **did** + **not** + the simple form of the main verb] in negative statements: *They did not write letters.*
- We use the negative contraction **didn't** for all subjects in conversation and informal writing.

Emma: *When I was a little girl, kids **made** fun of me. It **hurt** a lot. But I **got** through it.*

Practice

1. Underline the regular past tense verbs. Circle the irregular past tense verbs.

Rebecca and Emma <u>visited</u> Mr. Wang at his store. They (spoke) to him about Vincent. They gave him the children's cards, and he thanked them. Emma told Mr. Wang about Officer Jones's visit. The children learned about prejudice. Emma also said something about her own experiences with prejudice. She and Rebecca hoped to see Vincent back at the after-school program.

2. Match the simple form and the simple past tense form of each irregular verb.

1. __c__ do   a. went   6. ____ have   f. read
2. ____ drive   b. found   7. ____ put   g. saw
3. ____ eat   ✓ c. did   8. ____ read   h. put
4. ____ find   d. drove   9. ____ ride   i. rode
5. ____ go   e. ate   10. ____ see   j. had

3. Write the irregular verbs in the correct places in the chart below.

begin-began	buy-bought	cost-cost	fight-fought	sit-sat	think-thought
bring-brought	catch-caught	cut-cut	hit-hit	spend-spent	win-won
build-built	come-came	drink-drank	send-sent	teach-taught	write-wrote

The simple form and the simple past tense form are the same.		The simple past tense form ends in *-aught* or *-ought*.		The simple form and the simple past tense form have different vowels.		The simple form ends in *-d* and the simple past tense form ends in *-t*.	
SIMPLE FORM	SIMPLE PAST TENSE FORM	SIMPLE FORM	SIMPLE PAST TENSE FORM	SIMPLE FORM	SIMPLE PAST TENSE FORM	SIMPLE FORM	SIMPLE PAST TENSE FORM
1. cut	cut	**1.** teach	taught	**1.** sit	sat	**1.** send	sent
2. cost	cost	**2.**		**2.**		**2.**	
3. hit		**3.**		**3.**		**3.**	
		4.		**4.**			
		5.		**5.**			
		6.		**6.**			

4. Write affirmative or negative statements in the simple past tense. Use words from the boxes.

I	We	get	take	a little money	a lot of money
He	You	read	win	many letters	the message
She	They	spend	write	a book	$100

1. I wrote the message (or) I didn't write the message.
2. _____
3. _____
4. _____
5. _____
6. _____

Practice

5. What did you do last summer? Write five affirmative and five negative statements in the simple past tense. Use irregular verbs. Use your own paper.

Examples: I had a good time. I didn't go to school.

SIMPLE PAST TENSE, *YES/NO* QUESTIONS AND SHORT ANSWERS (IRREGULAR VERBS)

YES/NO QUESTIONS			AFFIRMATIVE SHORT ANSWERS			NEGATIVE SHORT ANSWERS			📝 NOTES
DID	SUBJECT	MAIN VERB	YES	SUBJECT	DID	NO	SUBJECT	DID + NOT	• Simple past **Yes/No** questions are the same for regular verbs and for irregular verbs. We use [**did** + subject + the simple form of the main verb]. • Simple past tense short answers are the same for regular verbs and for irregular verbs. We use [**Yes** + subject + **did**] or [**No** + subject + **did** + **not** or **didn't**].
Did	I we you they he she it	win?	Yes,	I we you they he she it	did.	No,	I we you they he she it	did not. didn't	

Did Vincent **bring** back the guitar?

Yes, he did.

Practice

6. Check (✔) the *Yes/No* questions with irregular verbs. You can look at the lists of irregular verbs on page 1 and page 2 of this episode for help.

1. ____ Did Vincent return to the after-school program?
2. ✔ Did he bring back the guitar?
3. ____ Did his mother speak with Emma?
4. ____ Did he see Alex?
5. ____ Did Alex and Vincent talk?
6. ____ Did Vincent say good-bye to the children?

7. Write *Yes/No* questions and short answers.

1. We rode our bicycles. Did you ride your bicycles? Yes, we did.
2. The shoes didn't cost much. _____
3. I found some keys. _____
4. She hurt their feelings. _____
5. I didn't do my homework. _____
6. Our team won the game. _____
7. My sister felt sick. _____

8. Complete these questions about the story. Write *Did*, *Was*, or *Were*.

1. _Did_____ Mrs. Wang come to the after-school program?
2. _____ she see Emma?
3. _____ Emma in her office?
4. _____ Mrs. Wang tell Emma the news?
5. _____ Vincent happy about his parents' decision?
6. _____ Vincent and Alex together again?

9. Change these statements to *Yes/No* questions. Write short answers.

1. They lost the game. _Did they lose the game? Yes, they did._
2. I wasn't in class yesterday. _Were you in class yesterday? No, I wasn't._
3. We saw a good movie. _____
4. He was upset at the news. _____
5. She taught English. _____
6. We spoke to them. _____

10. PRETEND: Today your friend had an important test in school. Ask about it. Write simple past tense *Yes/No* questions.

1. you / take / your test — _Did you take your test?_
2. it / be / hard — _Was it hard?_
3. it / be / a long test — _____
4. you / have / any trouble with it — _____
5. you / do / well on it — _____
6. you / be / glad to finish it — _____

Practice

11. PRETEND: Write a conversation between you and your friend. Your friend went out last night, and you didn't. Write *Yes/No* questions in the simple past tense. Use irregular verbs. Make your conversation ten lines long or more. Use your own paper.

Examples: (name): *Did you have a good time last night?*
(name): *Yes, I did. I saw a movie.*
(name): *Was it good?*

SIMPLE PAST TENSE, WH- QUESTIONS AND ANSWERS (IRREGULAR VERBS)

WH- QUESTION WORD	DID	SUBJECT	MAIN VERB	ANSWERS
Who / Whom	did	you	see?	Diana.
What		he	do?	He built houses.
When		she	leave?	An hour ago.
Where		they	eat?	In the cafeteria.

NOTES
- Simple past tense **Wh-** questions are the same for regular verbs and for irregular verbs. We use [**Wh-** question word + **did** + subject + simple form of the main verb].
- We use **Who** in conversation and in informal writing. We use **whom** in formal writing and in formal speaking.

Where did Rebecca **go**?
She **went** to Vincent's house.

Practice

12. Match these past tense **Wh-** questions and their answers. Write the letters.

1. _b_ What did Rebecca tell Alex?
2. ____ What did Rebecca say to Ramón?
3. ____ Who did Alex go home with?
4. ____ Where did Rebecca go?
5. ____ When did she go there?

a. To Vincent's house.
✔b. She told him news about Vincent.
c. His father.
d. Right after work.
e. "I want to give Alex and Vincent guitar lessons."

13. Write **Wh-** questions in the simple past tense.

1. where / you / buy / that shirt — Where did you buy that shirt?
2. what / they / get / for lunch ____
3. when / she / hurt / her back ____
4. where / I / leave / my keys ____
5. who / you / meet / at the station ____
6. when / he / hear / the news ____

14. Write past tense **Wh-** questions about the missing information.

1. I saw . . . at the party.   Who did you see at the party?
2. We had . . . for dinner.   _____
3. He went to . . .   _____
4. She left at . . . :00 p.m.   _____
5. I wore . . . to the wedding.   _____
6. He took . . . to the restaurant.   _____
7. They said, " . . ."   _____

15. Complete these past tense questions. Write **did, was, were**.

1. Where _did_ he sit?
2. Who _____ you meet?
3. When _____ the appointment?
4. What _____ they send?
5. Where _____ your keys?
6. When _____ it begin?
7. Who _____ at the door?
8. What _____ it cost?

POWER Practice

16. PRETEND: Your neighbor went on a vacation last month. Write **Wh-** questions for your neighbor about his/her vacation. Use the simple past tense. Use irregular verbs from the list in the box.

Examples: Who did you go with?   When did you come back?

| go | come | see | do | eat | sleep | leave | have |

1. _____
2. _____
3. _____
4. _____
5. _____
6. _____

17. PRETEND: Your friend just came back from shopping. Write four **Wh-** questions and four **Yes/No** questions for your friend. Use the simple past tense. Use regular and irregular verbs. Use your own paper.

Examples: Where did you go shopping?   Did you buy clothes?

EPISODE 21 page 6

Episode 22 Guitar Lessons

SHOULD AND MUST: AFFIRMATIVE AND NEGATIVE STATEMENTS; YES/NO QUESTIONS AND SHORT ANSWERS

	SUBJECT	SHOULD/MUST	MAIN VERB
AFFIRMATIVE STATEMENTS	They He	should	exercise.
		must	pay taxes.
NEGATIVE STATEMENTS	They He	should not / shouldn't	smoke.
		must not / mustn't	drive fast.
	SHOULD/MUST	SUBJECT	MAIN VERB
YES / NO QUESTIONS	Should	we he	study?
	Must		pay taxes?

SHORT ANSWERS		
Yes,	we he	should. must.
No,	we he	should not. shouldn't. must not. mustn't.

NOTES
- We use **should** for advice or recommendation. There is a choice: *You should eat more fruit every day. They shouldn't drink and drive.*
- We use **must** for necessity. There is no choice: *She must pay taxes. We mustn't be late.*
- We use [subject + **should / must**] or [subject + **should / must + not**] in short answers.
- The forms of **should** and **must** are the same for all subjects.

Mrs. Mendoza: *First you **must** pick up all the popcorn. Then you **should** do your homework.*

Practice

1. Underline *should/shouldn't*. Circle *must/must not*.

1. Christine <u>should</u> move to Los Angeles.
2. Alex (must) go to school. It's the law.
3. Alex <u>shouldn't</u> go with his mother. He <u>should</u> stay with Ramón.
4. Alex (must not) drive a car. He's too young.
5. The Mendozas <u>shouldn't</u> sell their restaurant.
6. Ramón (must not) quit his job. He needs to make money.

2. Circle the answers.

1. Parents should / (must) feed their children.
2. Children <u>should / must</u> be good.
3. Children <u>should / must</u> do their homework.
4. We <u>should / must</u> pay our taxes.
5. They <u>should not / must not</u> be rude.
6. Teachers <u>should / must</u> help students.
7. Babies <u>should / must</u> have a lot of sleep.
8. Children <u>shouldn't / mustn't</u> play with fire.

3. Write six questions with *should* or *must*.

1. English / should / I / speak / every / day — Should I speak English every day?
2. you / leave / must / now _____
3. they / guitar / take / lessons / should _____
4. Rebecca / study / must / a lot _____
5. today / Pedro / should / work _____
6. children / must / school / go / to _____

4. Answer these questions.

1. Should people eat healthy food? Yes, they should.
2. Must you work? _____
3. Should children drive cars? _____
4. Must parents take care of their children? _____
5. Must police officers wear uniforms? _____
6. Should you do your homework? _____

Power Practice

5. Make two lists for yourself. Write three things that you *should* do and three things that you *shouldn't* do.

Examples: I should exercise every day. I shouldn't eat junk food.

I should: I shouldn't:

_____   _____

_____   _____

_____   _____

6. Think about students in your country. Write five sentences with *must* or *must not* and the phrases in the box. Use your own paper.

Examples: Students must wear uniforms. (or) Students must not talk to each other.

wear uniforms	listen to their teachers	watch a lot of television
do their homework	go to the library	talk to each other	talk to their teacher

COMPOUND SENTENCES WITH *AND*, *TOO*, AND *EITHER*

AFFIRMATIVE	+	AFFIRMATIVE	
I like him,	and	she does	too.
He left,		they did	
You are happy,		we are	
NEGATIVE	**+**	**NEGATIVE**	
She isn't here,	and	he isn't	either.
They don't go,		we don't	
I shouldn't work,		you shouldn't	

📝 NOTES

- We connect two affirmative clauses with **and** and **too**: *I have a dog, and she does too.*
- We connect two negative clauses with **and** and **either**: *He didn't speak Chinese, and they didn't either.*
- We use a comma before **and**.

Alex is working, **and** Ramón is **too**.

Practice

7. Write *A* next to each affirmative sentence. Write *N* next to each negative sentence. Underline *too*, and circle *either*.

1. __A__ Rebecca was happy, and Mrs. Wang was <u>too</u>.
2. __N__ Rebecca can't speak Chinese, and Ramón can't (either).
3. _____ Vincent can play baseball, and Alex can too.
4. _____ Vincent is excited about the guitar lessons, and Alex is too.
5. _____ Ramón doesn't want to go to Los Angeles, and Alex doesn't either.
6. _____ Mrs. Mendoza takes care of Alex, and Ramón does too.

8. Match the first and second clauses of each sentence. Write the letters.

1. __d__ She doesn't like hot dogs, and   a. he can't either.
2. _____ They needed some help, and   b. you shouldn't either.
3. _____ He shouldn't watch television, and   c. she should too.
4. _____ She can't play tennis, and   ✔ d. I don't either.
5. _____ David should study every day, and   e. we did too.

9. Combine these sentences with *and* and *too*.

1. Rebecca likes baseball. Ramón likes baseball.

   <u>Rebecca likes baseball, and Ramón does too.</u>

2. Alex is going to take guitar lessons. Vincent is going to take guitar lessons.

3. Ramón was at the picnic. Rebecca was at the picnic.

4. Alex made a card for Vincent. The other children made cards for Vincent.

5. Ramón can speak Spanish. Alberto can speak Spanish.

10. Combine these sentences with *and* and *either*.

1. We didn't like the movie. They didn't like the movie.

   We didn't like the movie, and they didn't either.

2. His class isn't small. Her class isn't small.

3. Sarah can't swim. Maria can't swim.

4. Tim shouldn't work hard. Marilyn shouldn't work hard.

Practice

11. What do you like? What do your friends like? Write three sentences with *and* and *too,* and three sentences with *and* and *either*. Use your own paper.

Examples: I like movies, and my friends do too. I don't like TV, and my friends don't either.

12. Compare yourself to your family. Write six sentences. Use your own paper.

Examples: I have black hair, and my brother does too. I'm not tall, and my father isn't either.

TAG QUESTIONS WITH *BE*, *SHOULD*, AND *CAN*

	AFFIRMATIVE STATEMENT		+	NEGATIVE TAG	
SUBJECT	BE			[BE + NOT]	SUBJECT
He	is	18,		isn't	he?
They	were	lucky,		weren't	they?
	NEGATIVE STATEMENT		+	AFFIRMATIVE TAG	
SUBJECT	[BE + NOT]			BE	SUBJECT
He	isn't	18,		is	he?
They	weren't	lucky,		were	they?

BE AS MAIN VERB

	AFFIRMATIVE STATEMENT		+	NEGATIVE TAG	
SUBJECT	SHOULD/CAN	MAIN VERB		[SHOULD + NOT]/[CAN + NOT]	SUBJECT
You	should	go,		shouldn't	you?
She	can	drive,		can't	she?
	NEGATIVE STATEMENT		+	AFFIRMATIVE TAG	
SUBJECT	[SHOULD + NOT]/[CAN + NOT]	MAIN VERB		SHOULD/CAN	SUBJECT
You	shouldn't	go,		should	you?
She	can't	drive,		can	she?

SHOULD/CAN

NOTES
- We form a tag question with [statement + tag]. The tag asks for confirmation about the statement.
- We use an *affirmative* statement + a *negative* tag.
- We use a *negative* statement + an *affirmative* tag.
- We use the tag *aren't I* after statements with *I am*.
- We use a comma before the tag and a question mark after it.

Rebecca: *You are excited about guitar lessons, **aren't you**?*
Vincent: *Yes, I am.*

Practice

13. Check (✔) the tag questions. Underline the tags.

1. ✔ Vincent can take guitar lessons from Rebecca, <u>can't he</u>?
2. ___ The boys should practice every day, shouldn't they?
3. ___ The lessons are free, aren't they?
4. ___ Should Alex move to Los Angeles with his mother?
5. ___ Ramón should talk with her about Alex, shouldn't he?
6. ___ Ramón isn't happy with the situation, is he?
7. ___ He can't make all the decisions about Alex, can he?
8. ___ Are Ramón and his ex-wife going back to court?

14. Match the sentences and their short answers. Write the letters.

1. __c__ You're going to go,   **a.** shouldn't they?
2. ____ Mary wasn't there,   **b.** is she?
3. ____ Patricia isn't rich,   ✔ **c.** aren't you?
4. ____ David and Marta should study,   **d.** can't he?
5. ____ He can swim,   **e.** are you?
6. ____ You aren't ready,   **f.** was she?

15. Add a tag question to each statement.

1. He shouldn't leave now, __should he__ ?
2. They can speak Spanish, _____ ?
3. The people aren't here yet, _____ ?
4. Japanese is a difficult language, _____ ?

16. Rewrite the incorrect sentences.

1. He can't go, can't he? __He can't go, can he?__
2. They were there, aren't they? _____
3. You shouldn't leave, can you? _____
4. We can hear them, can we? _____
5. The children shouldn't go home, shouldn't they? _____

Power Practice

17. Ask advice about learning English. Write ten statements with tag questions. Use the phrases in the box. Use your own paper.

Examples: Vocabulary cards are helpful, aren't they? I should watch TV in English, shouldn't I?

English newspapers	vocabulary cards	watch TV in English
speak English a lot	learn five new words a day	learn to use a dictionary
learn English quickly	speak in my native language	be patient
a tape recorder	talk to friends	talk to strangers
a mirror	practice writing	

Episode 23 — THE RETIREMENT PARTY

THE FUTURE WITH WILL: AFFIRMATIVE AND NEGATIVE STATEMENTS

AFFIRMATIVE STATEMENTS			
SUBJECT	WILL	MAIN VERB	
I We You They He She It	will	write see visit help	her tomorrow.

AFFIRMATIVE CONTRACTIONS
[SUBJECT + WILL]
I'll we'll you'll they'll he'll she'll it'll

NEGATIVE STATEMENTS			
SUBJECT	WILL + NOT	MAIN VERB	
I We You They He She It	will not won't	write see visit help	her tomorrow.

NOTES
- We use [subject + will + main verb] to talk about the future.
- The affirmative contraction for **will** is **'ll**.
- The negative contraction for **will not** is **won't**.
- We use **will** for all subjects.

Ramón: *Your mom **will move** to Los Angeles soon.*

Alex: *I **won't** go!*

Practice

1. Underline the word *will*. Circle the word *won't* in the sentences below.

1. Alex's mother <u>will</u> move to L. A.
2. Alex (won't) go with his mother.
3. Ramón won't move to L. A.
4. Rebecca will go to the retirement party.
5. Bill won't go to the party with Rebecca.
6. Rebecca will have fun at the party.

2. Change the sentences to negative.

1. I'll see you tomorrow. I won't see you tomorrow.
2. We will visit them soon. _____
3. They will call us today. _____
4. She'll tell him the answer. _____
5. You'll like this movie. _____
6. He will help you. _____
7. It'll be good. _____

EPISODE 23 page 1

3. Change the full forms to contractions in these sentences.

1. We will help you study. We'll help you study.
2. I will pick them up at 6:00. _____
3. He will not tell me the truth. _____
4. She will be happy to see us. _____
5. They will not have enough money. _____
6. You will not want these apples. _____
7. It will rain tomorrow morning. _____

Power Practice

4. What are your affirmative predictions for the year 2080? Write six sentences with *will*. Use the affirmative contraction for *will*.

Example: We'll live on the moon.

1. _____
2. _____
3. _____
4. _____
5. _____
6. _____

5. What are your negative predictions for the year 2080? Write six sentences. Use the negative contraction for *will*.

Example: We won't have wars.

1. _____
2. _____
3. _____
4. _____
5. _____
6. _____

THE FUTURE WITH *WILL*: *YES/NO* QUESTIONS AND SHORT ANSWERS; *WH-* QUESTIONS

YES/NO QUESTIONS			
WILL	SUBJECT	MAIN VERB	
Will	I we, you, they he, she, it	see	them?

SHORT ANSWERS		
YES/NO	SUBJECT	WILL/WON'T
Yes,	I we, you, they he, she, it	will.
No,		won't.

NOTES
- **Will** comes before the subject in **Yes/No** questions and in **Wh-** questions: *Will you be there? When will you be there?*
- Short answers have [**Yes** or **No** + subject + **will** / **won't**].
- The question words **Where, When, Who, Whom,** or **What** come before **will** in **Wh-** questions: *When will I see them? What will you do tomorrow?*
- We use **Who** in conversation and in informal writing. We use **Whom** in formal writing and in formal speaking.

WH- QUESTIONS				
WH- QUESTION WORD	WILL	SUBJECT	MAIN VERB	
Who Whom	will	I we, you, they he, she, it	meet?	
What			do?	
When			see	them?
Where			eat?	

Rebecca: **Will** you **go** to a retirement party with me?

Bill: *No, I* **won't.**

Practice

6. Underline the *Yes/No* questions. Circle the *Wh-* questions.

1. <u>Will Rebecca have fun at the party?</u>
2. (When will she go?)
3. Will the Mendozas get a lot of presents?
4. Where will Alex's mother move?
5. Will Ramón move too?
6. When will Alberto pick Rebecca up?
7. Will Alex go to the party?
8. Who will Rebecca see at the party?
9. What will Rebecca do at the party?
10. Where will the party be?

7. Match the questions and short answers.

1. __d__ Will the Mendozas go to France for Christmas?
2. ____ Will Rebecca dance at the party?
3. ____ Will Alex dance with Rebecca?
4. ____ Will the party be fun?
5. ____ Will Rebecca dance with Mr. Mendoza?
6. ____ Will the Mendozas like retirement?

a. No, he won't.
b. Yes, they will.
c. Yes, it will.
✓ d. No, they won't.
e. Yes, she will.
f. No, she won't.

8. Complete the questions with *When*, *Where*, *Who,* or *What*.

1. <u>When</u> will class begin? It will begin at 7:30.
2. _____ will we go for vacation? We will go to California.
3. _____ will we do after class? We will do our homework.
4. _____ will we call? We will call John.
5. _____ will you help me? I'll help you next Tuesday.
6. _____ will you know the answer? I'll know the answer after I read the book.
7. _____ will they live next year? They'll live in an apartment building next year.
8. _____ will she visit in the summer? She'll visit her family.
9. _____ will we have dinner? We'll have dinner in a restaurant.
10. _____ will we eat for dinner? We'll eat chicken and potatoes.

POWER Practice

9. Will your friend do anything special for his or her next vacation? Write two *Yes/No* questions, two questions with *When*, and one question with *Where*.

Examples: Will you go far away for your vacation?
When will you go on vacation?
Where will you go on vacation?

1. _____
2. _____
3. _____
4. _____
5. _____

10. Write your friend's answers to the questions in Exercise 9. Use affirmative and negative contractions for *will*.

1. _____
2. _____
3. _____
4. _____
5. _____

PRESENT CONTINUOUS TENSE AND SIMPLE PRESENT TENSE FOR FUTURE MEANING

PRESENT CONTINUOUS FOR FUTURE MEANING			SIMPLE PRESENT FOR FUTURE MEANING			NOTES
SUBJECT	VERB	ADVERB / PREPOSITIONAL PHRASE	SUBJECT	VERB	ADVERB / PREPOSITIONAL PHRASE	• We can use the present continuous tense and the simple present tense for the future: *I am leaving tomorrow. We have a date on Tuesday.*
I	am	tomorrow. soon. next week. in two weeks. next year.	I We You They	leave	tomorrow. soon. next week. in two weeks. next year.	• We usually use an adverb or prepositional phrase for future time: *She meets Rafael next week. He's graduating in 2004.*
He She It	is	leaving				
We You They	are		He She It	leaves		

Carmen: **We're going** to Mexico soon.

Alice: *That's great!*

Practice

11. Circle the correct verb forms.

1. Mr. and Mrs. Mendoza (are) / is going to Mexico soon.
2. They are / is visiting relatives on their trip.
3. Alice go / goes back to Phoenix after the party.
4. Alberto and Ramón am / are making a speech in a little while.
5. The party end / ends at midnight.

12. Complete the sentences. Put the verbs in parentheses in the simple present.

1. (leave)   I ___leave___ for college next week.
2. (go)   She _____ back to work tomorrow.
3. (have)   John and Steven _____ a test at the end of the class.
4. (end)   The movie _____ in two hours.
5. (meet)   The committee _____ next Wednesday.
6. (return) He _____ home in three months.

13. Put the words below in the correct order. Write sentences.

1. we / to / going / in / are / Florida / February   We are going to Florida in February.
2. is / us / month / visiting / he / next   _____
3. work / home / they / after / coming / are   _____
4. leaving / minutes / I / in / am / ten   _____
5. is / tomorrow / party / she / a / having   _____
6. working / you / tomorrow / are / night   _____

Power Practice

14. What are your plans for next weekend? Write eight sentences. Use present continuous and simple present for future meaning.

Examples: I'm going to the movies on Saturday.
            I have a date on Friday night.

1. _____
2. _____
3. _____
4. _____
5. _____
6. _____
7. _____
8. _____

15. Answer these questions with your own ideas. Use adverbs or prepositional phrases to show *when* in the future.

Example: When are you going home? I'm going home next month (or) I'm going home in one month.

1. When are you going on your next vacation? _____
2. When do you go back to work? _____
3. When do you finish this course? _____
4. When are you visiting your family? _____
5. When are you buying your next car? _____
6. When are you seeing your best friends? _____

Episode 24 — THE PHONE CALL

HAVE TO: PRESENT TENSE, AFFIRMATIVE AND NEGATIVE STATEMENTS; YES/NO QUESTIONS AND SHORT ANSWERS

	DO	SUBJECT	HAVE TO	MAIN VERB
AFFIRMATIVE STATEMENTS		I, We, You, They	have to	go.
		He, She, It	has to	
NEGATIVE STATEMENTS		I, We, You, They	don't have to	
		He, She, It	doesn't have to	
YES/NO QUESTIONS	Do	I, we, you, they	have to	go?
	Does	he, she, it		

SHORT ANSWERS			
YES/NO	SUBJECT	DO	
Yes,	I, we, you, they	do.	
	he, she, it	does.	
No,	I, we, you, they	don't.	
	he, she, it	doesn't.	

📝 NOTES
- We use the affirmative forms of **HAVE TO** for necessity: *I have to go home. She has to pay taxes.*
- We use the negative forms **don't have to** or **doesn't have to** when something is **not** necessary: *You don't have to go now. He doesn't have to sing.*
- We use **do/does** or **don't/doesn't** for short answers.
- **HAVE TO** has the same forms in the present and the future: *I have to go now. I have to go tomorrow. He has to pay now. He has to pay tomorrow.*

Alex: *I **have to** move to Los Angeles.*

Practice

1. Underline the affirmative verb forms of **HAVE TO**. Circle the negative verb forms.

1. Alex <u>has to</u> move to Los Angeles.
2. Alex (doesn't have to) call Rebecca "Ms. Casey."
3. Nancy and Angela <u>have to</u> speak to Rebecca.
4. Rebecca has to call her brother in Boston.
5. Alberto doesn't have to go to the airport.
6. Alberto and Rebecca have to say good-bye.

2. Circle the correct form.

1. Alan (doesn't have to) / don't have to take French next year.
2. My little brother <u>has to</u> / have to wear glasses.
3. I has to / <u>have to</u> practice the piano now.
4. Linda <u>has to</u> / have to go home at six o'clock.
5. They're rich. They doesn't have to / <u>don't have to</u> work.
6. You and I has to / <u>have to</u> talk.

3. Write *Yes/No* questions with **HAVE TO**.

1. the / kids / study this weekend   Do the kids have to study this weekend?
2. Ellen / find a job soon   _____
3. I / cook dinner now   _____
4. Sally and Ben / clean the house   _____
5. you / take care of the baby   _____
6. Keiko / practice basketball   _____

POWER Practice

4. Plan a party. Write one thing you have to do and one thing you don't have to do for each verb: *invite, buy, cook, think, call*.

Examples: I have to think about music for my party.
I don't have to think about games.

I have to . . .

1. _____
2. _____
3. _____
4. _____
5. _____

I don't have to . . .

6. _____
7. _____
8. _____
9. _____
10. _____

5. Write about your family members. Write five things they have to do. Write five things they don't have to do. Use your own paper.

Examples: My brother has to take out the garbage.
My grandparents don't have to work.

HAVE TO: PAST TENSE, AFFIRMATIVE AND NEGATIVE STATEMENTS; YES/NO QUESTIONS AND SHORT ANSWERS

	DO	SUBJECT	HAVE TO	MAIN VERB
AFFIRMATIVE STATEMENTS		I, We, You, They He, She, It	had to	go.
NEGATIVE STATEMENTS		I, We, You, They He, She, It	didn't have to	
YES / NO QUESTIONS	Did	I, we, you, they he, she, it	have to	go?

SHORT ANSWERS		
YES/NO	SUBJECT	DO
Yes,	I, we, you, they he, she, it	did.
No,	I, we, you, they he, she, it	didn't.

NOTES
- We use the affirmative form **had to** for necessity in the past: *It was late. I had to go home.*
- We use the negative form **didn't have to** when something was **not** necessary in the past: *You didn't have to go home. It was Saturday.*
- We use **did** or **didn't** for short answers.

Nancy got a phone call from Boston.
Then she **had to** find Rebecca.

Practice

6. Underline *had to* + the main verb. Circle *didn't have to* + the main verb.

Ramón <u>had to make</u> a cake for the party. Alex helped him, and it was a beautiful cake. Mr. Mendoza spoke at the party. They (didn't have to sell) the restaurant. They wanted to keep it. Ramón was very happy. Alberto had to smile, but he wasn't happy. Next, Mrs. Mendoza had to speak. Then Alberto and Ramón had to toast their parents. Then they all ate the cake and danced. Rebecca danced with Ramón. They were happy and they didn't have to talk very much. They danced for a long time. Then Nancy came to the restaurant. She had to speak to Rebecca. The party was over.

7. Change the affirmative sentences to negative.

1. I had to call home last night. *I didn't have to call home last night.*
2. We had to take a taxi. _____
3. Roland had to take the test. _____
4. Lazlo had to buy a new phone. _____
5. Carlos and Anita had to go to Puerto Rico. _____
6. Ellie had to work yesterday. _____

8. Change the statements to *Yes/No* questions. Write short answers.

1. You didn't have to eat alone. <u>Did you have to eat alone? No, I didn't.</u>
2. The train didn't have to stop. _____
3. Akito and Setsuko had to study last night. _____
4. José didn't have to practice after school. _____
5. The plane had to wait for one person. _____
6. Julia's boyfriend had to mail a letter. _____

POWER Practice

9. Write five sentences about things that you *had to* do in 1990-1995.

Example: I had to wash the dishes.

1. _____
2. _____
3. _____
4. _____
5. _____

Now write five sentences about things that you *didn't have to* do in 1990-1995. Then write one more sentence about each thing.

Example: I didn't have to buy car insurance. I didn't have a car.

6. _____
7. _____
8. _____
9. _____
10. _____

10. PRETEND: Your homework isn't finished. Write five excuses with *had to*. Use your own paper.

Example: I had to go to the doctor.

COMPOUND SENTENCES WITH OR

CLAUSE 1	OR	CLAUSE 2
They watch TV,	or	they read.
He went to the country,		he went to New York.
Do you want to see a movie,		do you want to stay home?
Is she going to go to college,		is she going to get a job?
Wait here,		come with me.
Call him,		write a letter.

NOTES
- We use **or** to connect two clauses with alternate ideas.
- The clauses can be statements, questions, or imperatives.
- We use a comma before **or** in compound sentences.

Rebecca watches the dancers, **or** she talks to Alex.

Practice

11. Check the compound sentences with *or*.

1. ✔ Alex sits alone at the party, or he helps his father.
2. ___ Rebecca talks to Alex, and he smiles.
3. ___ Alex will stay with Ramón, or he will go with his mother.
4. ___ Rebecca danced with Alberto, or she danced with Ramón.
5. ___ Rebecca and Ramón talk about Alex, but they don't talk about Alberto.
6. ___ Alberto will go to the airport, or he will stay at the party.

12. Change the statements to questions.

1. I can wear your sweater, or I can wear Bill's jacket _____
   Can I wear your sweater, or can I wear Bill's jacket?

2. There's a bus, or there's a train. _____

3. You drive, or you take the subway. _____

4. That's the phone, or it's the TV. _____

5. They started late, or the traffic was bad. _____

6. The kids should take a nap now, or they should go to bed early. _____

13. Put the words in the correct order. Write alternative imperatives with *or*.

1. come in / go out / or   *Come in, or go out.*
2. buy / make / or / the cookies / them   _____
3. a / call / letter / or / write   _____
4. or / paper plates / the dishes / use / wash   _____
5. a friend / on / or / stay / swim / the beach / with   _____
6. a piece of paper / in / or / the answers / use / write / your book

_____

Power Practice

14. Write statements about alternatives. Write six sentences about you or people in your life. Use *or* and the words in the box.

| for breakfast | after school | at night | on birthdays | on vacations | on weekends |

Examples: *I have coffee and toast for breakfast, or I have have cereal, eggs, and fruit.*
My brother plays basketball after school, or he does his homework.

1. _____
2. _____
3. _____
4. _____
5. _____
6. _____

15. Write six questions about alternatives for people in your life. Use *or*. Use the past, present, or future with the words in the box. Use your own paper.

| in elementary school | this morning | in the morning |
| in your free time | in the future | on your next vacation |

Examples: *Were you a good student in elementary school, or were you a bad student?*
Do you take your shower in the morning, or do you take it at night?
Will you get married in the future, or will you stay single?

Harris County Public Library
Houston, Texas